"John DiJulius provides many practical tips and techniques to achieve the elusive goal of consistent service excellence. *Secret Service* has important lessons for any business that depends on personalized customer service for its competitive advantage."

—Alan Rosskamm, President & CEO, Jo-Ann Stores, Inc.

"[T]his book is full of forward-thinking ideas and promotional activities that can be implemented in short order. If you are looking for ways to create energy in your business, this book will be your guide."

—Fredric J. Holzberger, President and CEO,
Fredric's Corporation

"Truly one of the best books ever written on providing 'real customer service' that works. If you want to create partnerships with customers so they keep coming back, then you have to read this exceptional book!"

—Marc Blaushild, Vice President, Famous Enterprises

"This book raises the standards of customer service. I made it a must-read for all my employees."

—Joe Pannitto, Branch Manager, United Rentals, Inc.

# Secret Service

# Secret Service

## Hidden Systems That Deliver Unforgettable Customer Service

**John R. DiJulius III**

## AMACOM

### American Management Association

New York • Atlanta • Brussels • Buenos Aires • Chicago • London • Mexico City
San Francisco • Shanghai • Tokyo • Toronto • Washington, D. C.

This publication is designed to provide accurate and authoritative
information in regard to the subject matter covered. It is sold with
the understanding that the publisher is not engaged in rendering
legal, accounting, or other professional service. If legal advice or other
expert assistance is required, the services of a competent professional
person should be sought.

Library of Congress Cataloging-in-Publication Data

DiJulius, John R., 1964–
    Secret service : hidden systems that deliver unforgettable customer service /
John R. DiJulius III.
        p.    cm.
Includes bibliographical references and index.
    ISBN-10: 0-8144-7171-4
    ISBN-13: 978-0-8144-7171-5
    1. Customer services.    2. Consumer satisfaction.    3. Customer loyalty.
    I. Title

HF5415.5 .D558 2002
658.8'12—dc2

                                                          2002014953

Printing number
20

*To Stacy, who has been an incredible partner, mentor, wife, lover, mother, role model, and best friend. Without you, this book would not exist.*

*To my boys, Johnni, Cal, and Bo, who are my best (male) friends and the joys of my universe. Your laughter can make everything else seem insignificant.*

*To the rest of my family who have always looked after, taken care of, and supported me.*

*To my mother who was a pillar of strength and never allowed any obstacles to dictate what she or her children could achieve.*

# Contents

# Foreword

There's a story about an aging Walt Disney who was in his studio one day and met a young boy, and it goes like this:

"Do you draw Mickey Mouse?" the boy asked.

"No, I don't draw any more," Disney replied.

"Do you make up all the jokes and ideas?"

"No, I don't do that either."

"Well, then, what do you do, Mr. Disney?"

After a thoughtful pause, Walt Disney smiled at the boy and said, "Well, sometimes I think of myself as a little bee. I go from one area of the studio to another and gather pollen and sort of stimulate everybody. I guess that's the job I do."

John DiJulius is the Walt Disney of John Robert's. In *Secret Service,* John demonstrates how the most effective leaders continuously strive to bring together the right people, give them the finest tools, and inspire them to deliver unforgettable customer service. They know that legendary customer service is not about smiles and simply being nice. It's about vision, systems, training, and creating a magical moment for each and every guest . . . becoming truly customer intimate.

*Secret Service* takes the reader behind John's best customer service practices to glimpse his personal experience in building a phenomenally successful hair salon and spa. He has totally redefined the salon experience, and as a result his organization is growing at an astounding rate of 1,000 customers a month, retaining almost 70 percent of new customers (twice the industry average) and (at the time of this writing) is operating in only three locations.

*Secret Service* is packed with stories of people delivering what is termed in most organizations as extraordinary service, but in companies like John Robert's, Disney, and The Four Seasons Hotels, these first-class behaviors are all in a day's work.

If you're in business today, you really have two choices: either you can decide to compete on price alone and hope you can maintain a cost structure to generate a profit, or you can provide magical moments that create value for your guests. Your customers can either view your product or service as a commodity that any one of your competitors can provide, or they can view it as a unique experience that only you can provide. Turning the concept into reality is where most leaders fail in the arena of customer intimacy. Throughout *Secret Service,* DiJulius demonstrates how to transform bland customer service standards into memorable customer experiences. There is great risk in doing nothing or in merely accepting mediocrity in the business of service, and no organization can afford this mentality for very long without incurring disaster.

Success comes from dreaming, believing, daring, and doing . . . the process attributed to Walt Disney and his world-class entertainment empire. It's a carefully wrought process that leaders like John and Stacy DiJulius have adopted and translated to their dedicated team members at John Robert's Spa. As the curious boy learned from Walt himself, this is what great leaders do . . . they stimulate others to achieve great things. In the following pages, you'll find that what worked for John Robert's and the world's most famous mouse can also work for you.

Enjoy.

Bill Capodagli and Lynn Jackson
Founders of Capodagli Jackson Consulting and coauthors of *The Disney Way: Harnessing the Management Secrets of Disney in Your Company,* and *The Disney Way Fieldbook*

# Preface: Impossible Dream versus Reality

In the 1980s the salon industry was very different from what it is today. Many salons were poorly run businesses, hairdressers jumped from salon to salon, and poor customer service was the norm. Clients accepted this state of affairs, and few customers respected their salon or its staff.

These salons didn't make much money or survive for long. Few offered their employees such benefits as hospitalization and vacation, let alone 401Ks or further education. Opportunities for advancement were rare. A hairdresser couldn't expect to advance to a better job; nor for that matter could a receptionist. As a result, many frustrated people sought greener grass at other salons that offered what often turned out to be false hopes and bogus opportunities. At that point, the employees often chose a totally new career.

My wife, Stacy, and I dreamed of creating a very different kind of salon business. We wanted it to have high ethical standards and to take the client's experience to a new level. We wanted to reward and recognize our team members in countless ways and to give them the same benefits and opportunities they could find in other industries. We wanted to contribute to our community, not just take money from it.

Our dream was basically to enhance the quality of the lives around us by being a wonderful place where customers love to come, by creating jobs that make people feel good about themselves, and by sharing our success with the community through contributions to significant causes. In our dream salon, the employees would be enthusiastic about coming to work, would take pride in what they did and in their company, and in the process would find a purpose that touched their lives as well as those of their clients.

It looked great on paper. To carry it out was such a huge challenge that it sometimes seemed impossible. We had to create this vision clearly so that we could measure real life against our ideal. We had to keep reminding ourselves that we were on the right path no matter how rough it got.

We had to ignore the voices of critics. We had to resist the temptation to follow industry tradition and cheat a little along the way; that might solve many of our problems in the short term, but we believed it would not be beneficial in the long run. We had to believe that if we built the business the right way and trusted others, we would eventually all benefit even more than we had originally hoped.

We had to walk the walk every single day, making sure we were what we said we wanted to be, and making sure we did everything with integrity. We had to revisit our mission and vision constantly to make sure we lived up to it, adjusting it and evolving rather than allowing ourselves to think that what worked yesterday would work today and tomorrow.

Above all else, I am proudest that with all the success of John Robert's and all the careers we have created, none of it happened at the expense of other salons. We owe our phenomenal success to the passion our core team has shown from the beginning. You don't need to rely heavily on rules and policy if you have a team of people who are totally engaged. Even now, with many more than 100 employees, that passion and family feeling are strong. Our core team shared our dream and faith and made John Robert's what it is today. Without our core team, we would be nowhere.

When I told others I was writing a book about customer service, I was overwhelmed by the number of people who wanted to share horror stories. When I asked for shining positive experiences, most people didn't have any. Why do we have so many bad stories and so few good ones? Are things really that bad today?

And if we already know that the most successful businesses in every industry are the ones that execute the highest levels of customer service, then why don't more than 5 percent of all businesses actually do it? Is it any wonder that nine out of ten companies go out of business in the first 5 years? My intention with this book is thus to help businesses create systems to improve and institutionalize outstanding customer service.

Even though it wasn't easy, I researched and persisted in my pursuit of companies that routinely execute great customer service. I discovered that customer service is not dead in America. I found many great companies that execute superior customer service on a consistent basis. Although these companies come in all shapes and sizes, from mom-and-pops to international firms, every one of them implements a Secret Service system of non-negotiable best practices.

In creating systems for John Robert's, we borrowed from and applied best practices of the leading companies all over the world. *Secret Service* includes many of these clever and often simple ideas. Learning from the best, we implement and manage systems to increase the percentage that every customer's encounter turns out to be a pleasantly surprising experience that ensures repeat business, increased dollars spent, and many referrals. In each chapter we show how these systems can easily be transferred to any other industry; you can implement these ideas in your own company.

*Secret Service* takes a serious look at the most important number a business can track: customer retention. By creating hidden systems that truly impress customers, you will see your retention rates soar. *Secret Service* explains how to:

- Create your Customer Experience Cycle for consistent customer service.
- Deliver legendary service.
- Maintain professionalism in your front line.
- Make your service an experience.

- Stimulate additional sales by going deeper with existing customers.
- Keep employees happy.
- Deal successfully with unhappy customers.

Every chapter has many examples of how companies in other industries provide or can provide Secret Service.

Every business needs to create behind-the-scenes systems that guide its employees to ensure they deliver unforgettable customer service and delight clients with pleasant surprises.

# Acknowledgments

While I had always dreamed of writing a book, I never realized how difficult it would be, or how rewarding. A great many people helped make this book a reality.

I have had the good fortune to have many great mentors and role models, wonderful colleagues, and an innate determination to be the best (some say it's a compulsion or obsession). When you add it all up, John Robert's has achieved more than I ever thought possible.

Because so many people have been so generous with their wisdom and experiences, I decided to share the best practices that have made John Robert's so successful. These best practices have worked for many types of companies, and they can help you enjoy more prosperity and fulfillment in your endeavors.

Every day for the past year I made Denise Thompson, Marketing Director, Mary Iacobucci, Office Administrator, and Melissa Voinovich, People Development Coordinator, stop what they were doing to listen to my ideas, research answers and sources, contact someone, or proof something I'd just written. Whenever I came across something new and didn't know the proper protocol, I had them figure it out. I could not have done this book without their help.

My management team has made it all possible: Kathy Cheyfitz, Guest Care Coordinator; Denise Thompson; Eric Hammond, Director of Operations; and Lisa Adams, Spa Director. They all believed in a dream and took big pay cuts to join John Robert's in the early days. Often their passion and drive equaled or surpassed my own. With no guarantees, only blind faith and unwavering determination, they took that dream and pursued it relentlessly to make John Robert's one of the premier salons and spas in the United States. I have learned to surround myself with brilliant people and hope that I will be guilty by association.

So many people were so generous with their help, especially Jim Gilmore, author of *Experience Economy;* Bill Capodagli, *The Disney Way;* Shep Hyken, *The Loyal Customer* and *Moments of Magic;* and Hal Becker, *Can I Have Five Minutes of Your Time?* and *Lip Service.* These four successful authors were an enormous resource. They spent countless hours answering my questions and providing contacts and priceless tips. I will never forget their generosity. I hope I can somehow return the favor and also be that kind of resource for others.

Fredric Holzberger, CEO of Fredric's Corporation, an Aveda distributor, has been an extraordinary mentor and friend. He taught me how to take care of customers like no one else I have ever met. He believed in me long before anyone else did or should have. He gave me my first opportunity as a speaker and consultant, and he propelled my speaking career into one that is sometimes more than I can handle.

Michael Blitz, a business consultant in Iowa, saw an article on us in 1996, interviewed me by phone, and came to Cleveland to film a documentary on John Robert's. He became our biggest fan way back when we were very small. He saw so much potential in us, probably more than I did. Few people had as much confidence in my ability. Over the years he has become a great resource and friend. Michael is the only person I know who is not at all surprised by all our success.

Many people read my manuscripts and gave me invaluable feedback. I can't thank these people enough for all their time and effort, and many of their ideas are incorporated into the final version. I thank everyone, particularly those who read the manuscript in its various versions: David and Susan Akers, Marc Blaushild, and Tracy Pavlish.

I am grateful to Ellen Kadin and all the people at Amacom Books who believed in me and this book. My editor, Florence Mustric, had the tall task of unscrambling all my ideas, cleaning up my grammar, and making me sound clever. I am very fortunate to have had such a wonderful editor to dive into this book with enthusiasm and passion to help it reach its fullest potential. She treated it like it was her baby. My English teachers said I would be in trouble later on in life if I didn't pay more attention in class—little did they know that I would have Florence to make me sound intelligent.

My wife, Stacy, and I are indeed fortunate to have such an outstanding staff. Many people complain about the work ethic and youth today. We have found the opposite to be true. So many people, age 18 to 75, are dedicated to us and John Robert's. They are motivated to show the greatness inside them. The best ideas in the world are worthless without a great team to execute them.

Most importantly, my wife, Stacy, has inspired me to want to be a better person every day. Without her, there would be no John Robert's to write about. It is her talents that built John Robert's up from nothing. Today she charges $100 for her haircuts and is booked out 10 weeks. Although I get most of the credit and publicity, anyone close to us knows she is the real genius and backbone of our company. It's not easy being married to me and holding down the fort when I work long hours, travel a great deal, and spend what little free time is left on this book. Through it all, as an incredible wife and mother, her patience, support, and confidence have made all the difference.

# CHAPTER 1

# Secret Service Systems:
## Creating Behind-the-Scenes Systems

> In the new world of fanatical customer service, even small companies never sleep and no request is too ridiculous. That intensity is evident among cutting-edge companies.
>
> —*Inc. Magazine,* April 2001

"Service in America today has never been worse." This is a quotation from a book on customer service written more than 25 year ago, and this feeling has been expressed in dozens of books published since then. Regardless of whether it is true that service continues to decline or our mindset is that customer service in America has reached its lowest point, there can be definite advantages to the public having a poor perception of customer service. The most important of these is that consumers are willing to pay a premium to have their needs met and that there is no limit to what they will spend if their expectations are consistently exceeded.

## Secret Service

*Secret Service* is the implementation of hidden systems that enable our staff consistently to exceed the client's expectations and to make the

1

client feel welcome, comfortable, important, and understood. These systems help companies create a solidly loyal customer base by implementing simple ideas that provide customer service that will be remembered. By managing these systems, companies turn most customer encounters into a surprisingly pleasant experience for the customer. The result is that repeat business is ensured, more dollars are spent, and many referrals are gained.

When we first opened John Robert's in 1993, we wanted to make our mark not only in the beauty industry but also in the business community. We didn't want to be another business with good intentions but poor execution that could not keep its promises.

A noticeable quality sets the Nordstroms, Ritz Carltons, and the Walt Disney Worlds apart from other companies that offer the same types of goods and services. Our goal was to be in their category, not a company with occasional great flashes, or one in which a percentage of employees merely walk the talk, but a company that exceeds customer expectations on a routine basis.

We started off in typical fashion, with an impressive philosophy and written mission statement, with the hopes that our staff would automatically observe them every day, every time. But as our employee numbers grew from 2 to 15 to 30 to 50 and then to 130, we found it very difficult if not impossible to provide a high level of service on a regular basis. It became obvious that we would eventually become an ordinary business that couldn't execute what it preached if we didn't find a way to create and manage systems that employees could consistently deliver. There could be no allowance for deviation. By creating Secret Service systems, we reduced the inconsistencies and gray areas that lead employees to rely on their personal interpretations.

## Establish Non-Negotiable Systems

Secret Service systems are non-negotiable in two ways. First, if created and managed in the right way, customer service becomes non-negotiable for employees, who must deliver it. Second, if we implement Secret Service consistently, then we become a non-negotiable entity in our customers' lives.

In a slower economy, people start to look for things they can cut out or cut back. When you deliver exceptional customer service regularly, you go from being a discretionary entity to a necessity. People put you on the list of things they cannot do without, along with food, rent, and utilities. We don't want to be considered discretionary, so it is vital that we deliver non-negotiable customer service.

When I started in the salon industry, one of the first things I learned was the dismal client retention rate throughout the business. How hard could it be for a salon to get a new client to return for a second visit? It turns out to be extremely difficult. The national average retention rate for salons is about 35 percent, which means that more than 6 out of 10 new clients do not return to that salon for a second visit. Given this statistic, how could salons keep their doors open? I learned that's exactly why a large number of salons go out of business every year.

At that time, in 1994, we had been open about a year. Like most salon owners, I assumed our retention rate was much higher, closer to 80 or 90 percent. We provided very good services and all our operators had been very well trained. We purchased a software system to track client retention, and the numbers weren't impressive: Our average retention rate was about 50 percent. I was sure something was wrong. After cross-checking the numbers, I realized that the computer data were true.

The trade magazines considered 50 percent acceptable and anything above 60 percent excellent. I couldn't accept 50 percent, however. At that time we were attracting 150 new clients a month, 1,800 a year (today we get about 1,000 new clients a month). A 50 percent retention rate meant we were turning off 900 people a year. Even more worrisome, if we were turning off 900 people, what were they saying about us? Furthermore, the cost of acquiring a new customer is estimated to be at least six times greater than that of retaining an existing one. And to think, our numbers were considered good in our industry.

## The Customer Experience Cycle

Clients want either the best or the least expensive; there is no in-between.

—David Wagner

At this point I realized that the service is about much more than a haircut. It is about an experience, especially at our prices. Even in those days, we were one of the more expensive salons. We provided great haircuts, but so did many other salons.

So we pondered, "What would make clients feel that our services were such a great value that previous salon and spa experiences would pale by comparison? How could we make everyone feel like a regular client?"

Our answer was to create and implement Secret Service systems that would become the foundation of our training program for all employees and would be just as important as their technical training. Plain and simple, we were creating a client-retention game plan that would help us get more clients to return to our salons on a regular basis. A major portion of our Secret Service systems is what we call the Customer Experience Cycle. This is the total experience, starting when the client first contacts us, continuing through the visit, and ending with our follow-up phone call a few days later.

Our entire team, 15 at that time, got together and started to brainstorm answers to some very specific questions: In a perfect world, what would we want clients to experience when they call us? What would we want clients to experience when they walk in the door? And so on.

That brainstorming led to our Secret Service systems. It is of key importance that everyone participates in its development. Not only do you get excellent ideas that you may not have thought of on your own, but you also gain employee buy-in. If we had walked in one day and told our staff, "This is the way everyone is going to start answering the phone and greeting our clients from now on," they would not have been open to it. Because their own ideas were implemented, our staff owned them and wanted to prove they were excellent concepts.

The foundation for the Customer Experience Cycle came out of this initial brainstorming event and we have used it ever since. We borrowed many ideas from our experiences with businesses in other industries, especially restaurants, hotels, and distributors. Every year we add new features to the Customer Experience Cycle to improve it. We identified the stages of every possible situation a client could encounter, and we brainstormed what we ideally want to happen at each stage of the cycle.

## Figure 1-1. Stages of the Customer Experience Cycle

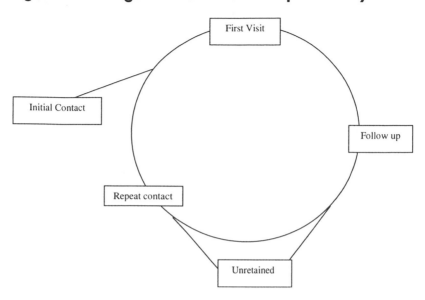

By looking closely at each stage, a company begins to develop perfect scenarios that it wants each customer to encounter and each staff member to execute. In the process of developing the Customer Experience Cycle, it's important to include seemingly wild ideas. Some of them will prove impractical, but many can be modified and implemented. The key is to have a realistic game plan that every team member can be expected to follow on a consistent basis.

The Customer Experience Cycle varies from business to business. In many businesses, the customer makes the first contact; in others, the company makes the first contact. The length of the cycle can be as brief as a few minutes or can extend over several months. Regardless of these differences, every business can identify the clear impression it wants to make at each stage of the customer's encounter. What do you want to happen the first time a client does business with you? Every business can develop its own Customer Experience Cycle. Develop an outline of your customer service cycle that will be expanded later. Here's an outline to get you started:

**Initial contact (preliminary, probably by phone)**
- Act in a professional and courteous manner.
- Reduce any anxiety and uncertainty caller may feel.
- Educate and inform the caller.
- Book the appointment (or close the sale).
- Provide an opportunity to schedule additional services.

**Delivery of first product or service**
- Act in a professional and courteous manner.
- Reduce any anxiety and uncertainty the client may feel.
- Create a truly friendly atmosphere.
- Provide a great experience.
- Exceed the client's expectations.
- Provide an opportunity to schedule another service.
- Give an impressive send off.

**Follow-up**
- Phone call
- Postcard
- Birthday card
- Newsletter

**If a client does not return (unretained client)**
- After 4 months: Send "We Miss You" card reminding that it's time for next appointment.
- After 8 months: Send an incentive to return, such as a 25 percent discount.
- After 12 months: Call to survey why the client never returned.

**If a client does return (retained client)**
- Recognize that client as a repeat customer.
- Repeat all steps of the initial contact stage.

It is easy and extremely beneficial to develop your Customer Experience Cycle. Include your staff in breaking down each interaction of your customers' contact with your company. Not only will your staff provide valuable insight and ideas, they will also take ownership of the new Customer Experience Cycle. Very few models will look the same; a retail store's model will be drastically different than a manufacturer's or auto mechanic's. Regardless, each will have the basic foundation, such as initial contact, activity of purchase/service, completion of the experience, follow-up, and hopefully repeat business.

Putting the Customer Experience Cycle on paper is the point at which many businesses stop. After creating a general model, they simply hope their staff will use good judgment and common sense. Common sense is, unfortunately, sometimes uncommon, and employees often find it easier to take the path of least resistance. Exceptional customer service is never easy.

Don't rely on the generalities of the model. Simply saying "Be professional and courteous," or "Reduce their anxiety" doesn't mean every employee will automatically know how to do this, or ensure that he or she will do it every time. So after you develop your outline for each stage of the customer encounter, break each stage down into smaller parts and identify specific objectives.

This removes personal interpretation, but it does not stifle creativity on the part of your employees, because you emphasize that the Customer Experience Cycle is the minimum you want each client to experience at each stage, not the maximum. If an employee wants to add to it or improve on it, that should be encouraged. The Customer Experience Cycle is meant to be a game plan to be followed consistently.

Here is a brief example of a Restaurant's Customer Experience Cycle.

### Pre-Experience: Reservation
- Fact finding information
- Find out what the occasion is, for example, promotion, anniversary, birthday.
- Schedule reservations.

### Start of the Experience
- Educate shift on this evening's event—who's coming in, VIPs, regulars, celebrations, and so forth, as well as their names and where these people will be located.

- Greet and acknowledge by every department—valet, hostess, and so forth.
- Utilize database if guest is a return customer—favorite drinks, appetizers, and so forth.
- If customers need to wait in the bar, have their favorite drinks ready for them.

**Experience**
- Warm and professional, customer is greeted by everyone who comes to the table
- Thorough and detailed presentation by the staff
- Additional acknowledgment by other staff members on guest's occasion, for example, several staff wishing them a happy anniversary

**Post-Experience**
- Smooth checkout
- Coat and valet ready for guest
- Cheerful sendoff
- Card sent out congratulating them on their occasion and thanking them for including ABC restaurant in their big night

As another example, here's a Customer Experience Cycle for one of John Robert's services. It identifies our intentions of what every client should experience when receiving a haircut at John Robert's.

**Pre-experience: provided by guest care personnel**
- Answer the phone enthusiastically, saying, "Thank you for calling John Robert's Mayfield (salon location). This is Kelly. How can I help you?"
- Allow plenty of time to answer all of the client's questions concerning services, the designers' credentials, availability, and so on.
- Give each client an opportunity to book appointments for additional services.
- Use the client's name at least four times during the call.
- Offer directions to the salon.
- Confirm the service, operator, time, and date.

- As the last thing before hanging up, say, "Is there anything else I can do for you?"
- Make a confirmation call to the client 24 hours before the appointment.

**Start of the experience: provided by hostess**
- Greet the client enthusiastically within 8 to 10 seconds.
- Confirm the client's appointment.
- Ask the client to fill out the information card.
- Immediately notify the operator of the client's arrival.
- Offer to hang up the client's coat and to provide a refreshment.
- Inform the client of any delays.
- Offer a tour of the entire facility.
- Show the client where the changing rooms are.
- Monitor the client's wait, and notify the operator again if the client is not taken within 10 minutes of the scheduled appointment.
- Use the client's name at least four times during the check-in.

**Pre-service: provided by designer**
- Provide consultation every time with every client.
- Show portfolio, analyze client's needs, and discuss client's expectations.
- Provide stress-relieving scalp massage.
- For men, provide a minifacial.
- Provide shampoo and conditioner.
- Use a white cape for new clients.

**Service: provided by designer**
- Give an excellent haircut.
- Massage hands and arms.
- Clean client's jewelry during massage.
- Keep the conversation on a professional level.
- Give lesson on blow-dry styling.
- Explain products used.

**Post-service: provided by designer**
- Touch up makeup for all female clients.

- Make client aware of additional services that salon/spa offers.
  - Give complimentary bang trim.
  - Inform client of complimentary blow-dry lesson in the future, to help the client duplicate it on her own.
  - Offer men complimentary neck and sideburn trimmings between visits.
  - Offer referral incentives: $5 gift certificate for every referral and contest with prizes for the clients who refer the most new clients during the year.

**Conclusion of experience: provided by various staff**
- Assistant, operator, and receptionist: Give client a friendly and enthusiastic sendoff.
- Designer and receptionist: Give an opportunity to purchase products used.
- Main operator: Give client a business card.
- Receptionist: Give client opportunity to schedule next appointment.
- Receptionist: New clients: Give client a new-client package that includes a menu of services, newsletter, business card, magnet, and five-question form. Inform client of 10 percent off next visit if she returns the completed form within six weeks.
- Receptionist: During check-out use client's name at least four times.
- Operator: Input personal information (such as name of spouse, children) in computer under client's name for use on future visits.

**Post-experience: provided by support staff**
- Client receives an enthusiastic phone call within 24 hours.
- Client receives a thank you postcard within 48 hours.
- Client receives a quarterly newsletter.
- Client receives a birthday card.
- If client has a challenge, handle it immediately on the spot. Make it right. Fill out customer challenge sheet and have management follow up.
- If client is not retained after 4 months: send out a reminder card that client is due for an appointment.

- If a client is not retained after 8 months: send out an incentive to return (such as 25 percent off for next visit).
- If a client is not retained after 12 months: survey with a letter or phone call to find out why.

For every service we have a Customer Experience Cycle. Many details are unique to each cycle, depending on whether it's a massage, manicure, or other service. Although it may seem like a great deal of additional work to develop and incorporate the Customer Experience Cycle and to create the required systems, the cycle eventually becomes second nature. Virtually everything in the Customer Experience Cycle is value added and provided at no extra charge, regardless of whether the client gets a $40 or a $100 haircut (the price is determined by the level of the designer).

Based on our analysis of the customer service cycle, we opened salon and spa facilities that are truly unique, not just in our region but also rivaling businesses anywhere in the United States. When you walk into our salon, you are greeted and checked in by a hostess who starts your experience. Instead of a traditional waiting area, which has a negative association, we feature an experience area where you can shop, test products, or purchase gift certificates.

Attached to the experience area is a café, where clients and team members can purchase lattes, cappuccinos, smoothies, salads, and sandwiches. A wall of fame displays the awards we have won and the feature articles written about us. Our main styling floor has 20 hair stations, used primarily for cutting and styling women's hair. We have a large nail area for all our nail services, and a private room where women have their hair colored, permed, and highlighted. Another private room is our men's salon, which features a pool table, sports memorabilia on the walls, stadium seats from the old Cleveland Browns Stadium, and a television tuned to ESPN or CNBC.

In this salon we have a totally secluded spa of 2,000 square feet. It features a big but cozy lounge; a pedicure room; leather massaging chairs; steam showers; and rooms for massages, facials, and wet treatments, such as mud packs and body wraps.

**Figure 1–2.   John Robert's annual sales, 1993–2001.**

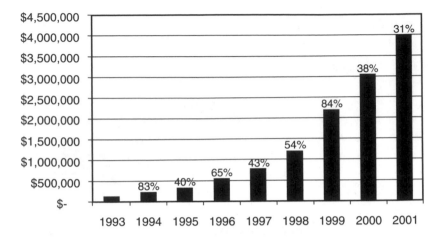

Finally, we have a fitness center of 1,000 square feet where we offer personal training. With this service, John Robert's has entered the wellness industry. It's safe to say that no other salon has so many unique amenities. We finally have the physical facility to complement the unforgettable customer service that built our business. Our Secret Service system has dramatically increased our growth and sales. Figures 1–2 and 1–3 document our annual growth in our first eight years (through 2001) in employees (from 2 to 130), in revenue (from $150,000 to $4 million), and in percentage of increase in sales (32% in 2001). We have

**Figure 1–3.   John Robert's employees.**

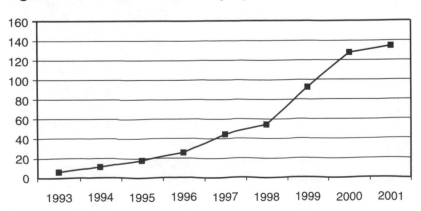

won nearly every award possible in our first eight years, including "Top 200 Salons in America" five years in a row; "Fastest Growing 100 Companies in Cleveland" five years in a row; and "Top 99 Companies to Work for in Northeast Ohio" four years in a row.

## Do the Small Things Right

This is Secret Service at its best. It's the small surprises that impress our clients and do more than anything else to increase our client retention dramatically. Complimentary extras increase loyalty. For example, Lube Stop allows customers to stop off any time between regularly scheduled oil changes and have their oil topped off at no charge. Car maintenance companies could also send a postcard or an e-mail reminder that it's time to make another visit. To send a reminder, the shop would simply have to identify the customers who were in three months ago, print labels, and send postcards once a week. That's a little work invested for a potentially large return. Other examples of great value added are free alterations of some high-end clothiers at any time—even a year after you purchased the garment.

The things clients enjoy most about coming to John Robert's are the scalp massage they receive before the shampoo, the hand-and-arm massage during the haircut, the makeup touch-up for women, and the minifacial for men during the shampoo. (Every hair station has a jewelry cleaner so clients can have their jewelry cleaned during the hand-and-arm massage.)

Clients also appreciate the free bang trims and clean-ups we offer any time between visits. Men find this especially helpful when they have an important appointment or interview for which they need to look their best. Women find the free blow-dry lesson helpful in showing them how to duplicate the look they received at the salon.

We offer all kinds of surprising little extras. For example, in the 2 weeks before Mother's Day we sell thousands of gift certificates, mostly to men who would then run to the nearest drugstore for a card. We eliminate the need for that errand by having a selection of Mother's Day cards to choose from. It's a small thing, but it contributes to a positive experience at John Robert's.

## Differentiate Between First-Time Customers and Return Customers

A perfect example of Secret Service is our white-cape system. On any day at John Robert's, we have about 16 clients in black capes and two or three in white capes. Clients are unaware of the fact, but the entire team at John Robert's knows the white cape signifies a new client. A staff member walking by may stop, welcome the client in a white cape to John Robert's, and ask her if she would like a magazine or a cup of coffee. A manicurist may introduce herself and say, "If you have time, I would love to give you a complimentary polish change." A client who has been welcomed by several team members instead of only her hairdresser is much more likely to return.

We know these value-added services are important because all new clients fill out comment cards before they leave. Those who recommend us to relatives, friends, co-workers, and others generally comment much more on the little frills they received than on the actual service.

One new client told me that she never had any intention of leaving her hairdresser at another salon until a co-worker spoke so highly about the John Robert's experience that her other salon seemed inadequate by comparison. This new client had paid $15 less for a haircut at her previous salon, but she didn't mind the higher price because of the way she felt after coming to us.

## Follow Through

A slogan without action is a lie. If not executed consistently, Secret Service can do more damage than good. Consider this scenario: A new client comes to John Robert's expecting a typical salon visit and is surprised by all the amenities she receives. She goes back to work and tells everyone how wonderful it was. A co-worker gets excited and schedules her next haircut at John Robert's, expecting all the frills she heard about, but receives only some of them. Consequently, she is disappointed, even angry, and complains to her co-worker. Now we have two disappointed clients, the one who received a less-than-excellent experience, and the one who hyped it up and now looks foolish. The first client came in with low to moderate expectations and we exceeded them, but the second came in with extremely high expectations and we underperformed. We must create checks and balances to ensure that we are as consistent as possible to prevent this scenario from happening.

The Customer Experience Cycle has been one of our most powerful Secret Service systems; since implementing it, our retention rate has soared, a sure measure of the success of our Customer Experience Cycle. Our retention rate is one of the best in the industry, about 70 percent compared with the industry average of 35 percent. Most of the extra things we do require very little time and money, but make our clients' experiences at other places seem pale by comparison.

High expectations apply to any service that consumes discretionary money and time, such as shopping and travel. All businesses compete for this time and money. Many businesses fuss a lot over outdoing the competition in their own industry, but in fact their most serious competitors are often in another industry. John Robert's competition is not just the salon across the street; it is any place where our clients and potential clients can choose to spend their time and money after weighing and comparing what they get.

There's an amusing story about perceptions that illustrates this situation. Two men were sleeping in a tent in the woods when they heard a ferocious bear clawing at their tent and trying to attack them. One of the men jumped up and started to put on his tennis shoes. The other man stayed in his sleeping bag and said, "What are you doing? You'll never be able to outrun that bear." The first man responded, "I don't have to outrun the bear. I just have to outrun you."

Clients spend their discretionary money wherever they have the best experience. We are busier than many of our salon competitors who charge a fraction of our prices. Why? Because we have made our clients feel they are getting a great value for their $100 haircut and that the salon charging only $25 may be overpriced. Very little of this perception has to do with the actual haircut.

Not only do we compete for the client's discretionary money, but far more important, we strive for our services to be viewed not as a discretionary item but as a necessity. We want to be considered an integral part of our clients' lifestyles, right up there with food and utilities. If we succeed, economic factors will not impact us. If we can continually exceed the client's expectations, then clients will view our company—not just our service or product—as a necessity in their lives.

The word "continually" is key. Whatever continually gives a client the most value—whether it's a weekend ski trip, shopping spree, or day of pampering at John Robert's—is what she will do with her available time and money.

Another vital aspect of providing Secret Service is how we keep our name in front of our clients. We mail birthday cards to all clients, telling them to come in and pick up the gift we have set aside for them, typically a trial size of a hair product of their choice. Every quarter, all clients receive a newsletter that updates them on what advanced education we have just completed, tells about our community involvement, profiles team members, and spotlights promotions and products. For clients we haven't seen in awhile, we send a "We miss you" card that offers some type of incentive for them to give us a try again. This has been particularly successful in regaining some clients who for one reason or another may not have planned to return to us.

## Treat Every Customer Like a Million Dollars

You never know who your customer is. Regularly test yourself to see how well you are performing every part of the Customer Experience Cycle. One way John Robert's does this is with secret shoppers, who are senior management students at local colleges. This is a profitable partnership in which the professor gets a real-life case study to use as a learning tool in his class, the students get a valuable service for free, and we receive valuable information that we can use to review our staff.

That information would be rewarding enough for us, but we receive an added benefit. These seniors are interviewing for jobs and starting their careers. They need to look their best while interviewing, and when they land new jobs, they earn more discretionary income than they have ever had. Our retention rate among these students is more than 50 percent.

How does our staff react to secret shoppers? We teach our staff about this process from the beginning, and secret shoppers are part of our culture. It's almost comical how hyper-aware our staff is; they perceive every client as a potential secret shopper. That alone keeps them on their toes. They will say to each other, "I think that was a secret shopper. Didn't she ask a lot of questions? Did you remember to do such-and-such?" Our secret shoppers have supplied information that we are able to use to improve all areas of our business.

Secret Service systems boost client retention dramatically. When you consistently exceed your client's expectations, you keep that client. It's that simple. As an added benefit, these clients are much more forgiving of any mistakes you may make.

## Refocus Your Team

It's harder to make your poor performers better than it is to make your goods ones great.

How can a company get its team to focus on the importance of always providing Secret Service and continually exceeding expectations? One important way is to make your staff constantly aware of their personal client retention rates.

Base everything on client retention. Here's how: When a staff member's retention rate reaches a certain level, she (or he) is promoted and her (or his) prices increase, which in turn results in an increase in income and certain benefits. In addition, a staff member's client retention rate determines how many new clients she (or he) will get each month. New clients who do not request a specific staff member should be referred to employees with higher retention rates.

Post all retention rates in the employee lounge every month. Every quarter print out for every staff member the entire list of new clients seen in the past 12 months, showing who has returned and who hasn't. As long as the client returns, the operator who saw the client first gets credit for retaining the client even if that operator never performs another service for the client. The objective is to provide the new client with an experience so pleasant that the client will want to do business with us again, regardless of who provided the service and what it was.

Secret Service Systems relate to every industry because each has customers, be they the public or other businesses. It doesn't matter whether you call them customers, clients, guests, patients, vendors, distributors, or tenants.

Aware of it or not, every business already has a Customer Experience Cycle. Your cycle is what routinely happens from the moment a client calls your company and receives a first impression on through everything that typically happens to the client from that point on. In most businesses the cycle unfortunately happens by accident rather than by design. It's important to emphasize that the Customer Experience Cycle is what typically happens, not what a business hopes will happen. The whole purpose of creating Secret Service systems is to ensure that what typically happens is what should happen.

The best of the best create their own Customer Experience Cycle. You can be a doctor's office or a graphic designer, a hardware store or a supermarket, a fast-food outlet or an upscale restaurant, a wholesale club or a boutique, a mass merchandiser, or a lemonade stand. Regardless of what you sell to whom and how, your customers go through an experience cycle every time they do business with you, whether it's every day, week, month, quarter, or year.

Every business needs to create behind-the-scenes systems that guide the employees to ensure that they deliver customer service that will be remembered as well as delight clients with pleasant surprises. Every business's Customer Experience Cycle will be different; even businesses in the same industry have dramatically different experience cycles. It's not the better company that wins; it's the company that manages the cycle, trains its people within its framework, and makes it a system that is written in stone, that (barring a natural disaster) is put in place every time with every client.

Let's say that most of your interaction with clients happens at your customer's location or by phone.

- What do you want to happen the moment they call you?
- How do you want your phone to be answered?
- What information should your person answering the phone be prepared with, such as prices, directions, and product information?

- What ideally do you want to accomplish with incoming calls? Do you want to schedule an appointment with a salesperson, direct the client to the best person during the initial call, or sell something on the spot?
- When you have the first face-to-face encounter with the customer, how do you want the encounter to unfold?
- What impression do you want to make?
- What support material do you want to provide?

Using questions like these will help you analyze every possible stage of the Customer Experience Cycle.

The most important part is the post-experience, but this is where many businesses fail to deliver excellent and consistent follow-up service. The activities are simple: sending a thank you card, including a gift of some sort as an incentive to do business again within a certain number of days, calling to see if the customer was completely satisfied, and continually putting your name in front of the customer as a reminder of what other services you offer.

**Guidelines for beginning your Secret Service System:**
1. Create Secret Service systems based on your Customer Experience Cycle.
2. Involve your entire staff in the process; let it be their innovation.
3. Never have a new employee interact with customers until he or she knows every stage of that cycle inside out.

This will provide consistent pleasant surprises that your customers will brag about.

## Examples of Exceptional Customer Service

*If you copy one person's stuff, it's called plagiarism;*
*if you copy fifty people's stuff, it's called research.*
*—Robert Shook*

For years I have scouted and analyzed examples of exceptional customer service in other industries and have found ways to apply successful techniques to my own business. We all need to do this constantly by asking ourselves three questions:

1. What Secret Service system is at work here?
2. Can this system somehow be tweaked and implemented in my business?
3. How can I make it a system that is executed 100 percent of the time?

One of my best dining experiences was a dinner to which my good friend and mentor Fredric Holzberger treated my wife and me at the Waterfront Restaurant in Cincinnati, Ohio. The food is outstanding and the service is even better. One detail is especially memorable. Even though the staff of the Waterfront made everyone feel special, they did a terrific job of making it obvious that Fred is a very good customer. Everyone knew him, and most of the staff made it a point to acknowledge him and the people in his party. For instance, he didn't even have to order wine. His favorite bottle was automatically brought to him, and it was labeled, "From the private stock of Fredric Holzberger." This kind of attention really leaves a good impression on the customer. Whether the Waterfront has a private stock or just prints a special wine label for a good customer and puts it on the bottle just before bringing it out, is a good example of a Secret Service System that creates loyalty.

Hotel concierges generally offer excellent customer service. You can call a fine hotel and arrange for the concierge to take care of virtually everything, from ordering flowers to a candlelight dinner to tickets for an event. Hotels can take Secret Service one step further and really make a difference. For instance, when you call to make reservations at a fine hotel, the hotel operator could also ask, "Is it a special occasion?" If you said yes, then he or she could say, "Would you like to upgrade to one of our romantic honeymoon suites?" or "Would you like our package that includes a suite, dinner, breakfast, and theater tickets?" or "Would you like me to connect you to our concierge, who has some great ideas to help make your anniversary very special?" This can be accomplished very simply, by training the hotel operators to incorporate that dialogue when making reservations.

Hotels could also contact you one or two months before your anniversary or your spouse's birthday to see if you would like to stay at their hotel again to celebrate the occasion. If the hotel has locations nationally, it could suggest a package at a resort site. This type of service would dramatically increase the likelihood of your using this hotel more often. All the hotel needs to do to implement this system is to manage on a monthly basis a database of customer preferences (ski slopes or beaches) and dates (birthdays and anniversaries). Many new age marketers are taking advantage of increasing computer databases and are utilizing the vast network of information in property management systems to understand their guests' wants and needs. This has been much more prevalent among the upscale properties, but the competition for the traveling consumer may force even the economy hotel brands to embrace breakthroughs in technology, such as database mining and frequent-user programs; if they do not, they may not be around for long. The hotel industry has a good opportunity, starting at check-in and continuing during the guests' stay, to create a detailed database that includes personal preferences and profiles. Having a captive audience for several days, the smart players will harness this information sitting in their database and deliver an unforgettable experience by anticipating guests' wants and needs, and deliver pleasant surprises that they didn't expect. Knowing who your consumer is gives you an advantage over your competition, from delivering a personalized experience to marketing to their future needs.

Every business can do a great deal to win loyalty and stimulate additional business. What kind of loyalty do appliance stores have? My wife and I rarely purchase more than one appliance from the same store because no store has made us loyal. Appliance stores can increase loyalty and sales by following up with customers so they think of that store first the next time they need another appliance. By providing great service and continuously informing customers about additional merchandise, sales, and special promotions, an appliance store would greatly increase the percentage of people who return, especially once that store has established that it can be trusted to offer a good product and deliver great service.

As an example, think of how much a family spends over the decades on furniture. Why don't more furniture stores continually market to their

existing customers, reminding them of the good quality they offer and informing them of all the types of furniture they sell? Instead, furniture
stores invest in huge amounts of advertising in newspapers and on radio
and television. The return on these ads can't begin to approach the return
on following up with existing clients. Again, this type of follow-up can
easily be done by executing strong systems with existing customers based
on when they last made a purchase (there's more on loyalty and additional business in Chapters 4 and 5).

Printers and advertising specialty firms have many opportunities
to stimulate additional sales. Because John Robert's give printers and
advertising specialty firms a great deal of business, they often recipro-
cate with holiday gifts, typically a gift certificate to a restaurant. How
effective it would be to give something that will stimulate new orders,
such as a small box of note cards that features my logo and company
name and says "Congratulations" or "Happy birthday" or "Happy anniversary." The owner could attach a note saying, "John, thank you so
much for calling me. I hope you enjoy this gift as a sign of my appreciation." On receiving this, I might immediately call and request 100 of
each card. Another great holiday gift would be a beautiful 9 × 12
pocket folder with the customer's company logo on it, along with a
small amount of the customer's stationary inside. Companies could
order a folder for all their managers and department heads because
employees look and feel so professional carrying around a beautiful
folder with the logo to hold their important paperwork. A thank you
gift of any product with a customer's logo would greatly increase the
chances of multiple sales because business owners love to see their
company name on things. In many cases, business owners want to see
all their employees or good customers wearing or using something
with the company's name and logo. So sending a gift accomplishes two
things. First, it shows that you appreciate their business or referral, and
second, it's a good opportunity to stimulate additional orders. Again,
this system can be created and managed easily.

## UPS

UPS has one of the top training programs in the world. I know because I drove for them for several years. They invest more time and

money in training their employees, and it shows in their continued success. First they train for safety, driving, as well as prevention of injury. Then they train for efficiency, and in this they excel, making UPS one of the most productive companies anywhere. Everything is timed, down to how you enter and exit your vehicle. Finally, they put enormous emphasis on customer service: how to take care of the customer, and go the extra mile. When they hear a story of an employee who has gone above and beyond, they celebrate it in front of all his or her coworkers and in their company newsletter, thereby stimulating the above and beyond culture. But most importantly, they do not train on safety, efficiency, and customer service only once a year; rather, it is part of their ongoing intensive training. They have a morning meeting before every shift; whether it's drivers, loaders, or others, the on-duty manager will discuss and remind them of their focus for the day. A few times a year each driver must have a safety ride. A safety supervisor will ride with the driver and ensure he is practicing and aware of all the safety systems that drivers are to use continuously, such as scanning mirrors and speedometers every 8 to 10 seconds, watching for stale green lights, and so forth. Because of the constant drills, drivers find themselves doing this all the time, any time they are behind the wheel. I haven't driven for UPS for more than 10 years and I still practice all their safety systems every time I step into a car. They continually retrain to foster that kind of culture in areas of efficiency and customer service as well. Their training has obviously paid off, because they are the number one leader in the package delivery business.

Pancho Thompson is a driver for UPS in Cleveland, Ohio, and probably one of the best the company has ever had. He takes out nearly twice the load of other drivers and consistently makes his run in less than eight hours, a feat he has performed day in and day out for more than 20 years, during which time he has also maintained a perfect safe driving record. He has mastered all of the great training UPS gives its drivers on how to reduce downtime for maximum efficiency. But productivity isn't what makes Pancho Thompson a great driver; what makes him exceptional is the way he continues to exceed his customer's expectations.

He once delivered a television stand to a house. In most areas a UPS driver can leave packages on the front porch and be on his way.

In this case, an elderly woman was waiting for Pancho at the door. The box was heavy, and he asked if she would like him to bring it in, and she said yes. After finding out that she lived alone, Pancho opened the box and assembled the stand for her, and he still ran early that day.

Of the systems a company creates, one of the most difficult involves creating a system for employees going above and beyond the call of duty because of the unpredictability of when such occasions will arise. The best way to create this system is to recognize constantly and celebrate the occasions when your employees achieve this, thus creating awareness and generally stimulating the human desire for public recognition. Doing this on every possible occasion—at meetings, on voice mail, and in your employee newsletters—fosters a culture in which employees want to extend that legacy.

## Hal Com Computers

Hal Com Computers, in Cleveland, does an excellent job of providing great service and at the same time stimulating more business. This company provides everything you possibly need. You can buy a new computer or printer from Hal Com, or get on-site same-day service, or buy troubleshooting hardware, software, networks, wiring, web hosting and design, or intranet services. Whatever you want or need, Hal Com can provide it, and they make you aware of that fact through many of the same vehicles described earlier.

I discovered Hal Com Computers when one of my computers was down and I needed it repaired immediately on-site. Someone recommended Hal Com, we called them, and within a few hours a technician arrived.

"Does Hal Com always come out the same day?" I asked.

"We can't always guarantee it unless you're a preferred customer. We not only guarantee our preferred customers same-day service, but they also get a better hourly rate, and we drop the service-call charge."

"How much do you have to spend to be a preferred customer?"

"It's not how much you spend. It's whether you use us exclusively for all your computer needs. You see, it wouldn't be fair to base it on how much you spend, because some companies are huge and have 500 computers, and some companies are small and have only six. If both companies give you all their business, then they both deserve priority service."

"How do you know a company is using you exclusively?"

"We trust them."

Hal Com offers one-stop shopping for all your technology needs, plus incentives. In addition, Hal Com contacts customers regularly to inform them when their computers need maintenance to prevent any problems before they happen. Hal Com also e-mails customers news about new versions of their software, the latest anti-virus updates, and new software that the customer doesn't have but might be interested in. As a result of all their in-your-face marketing as well as their exceptional service and incentives, the customer will want to give Hal Com all his or her computer business. Again, Hal Com is able to accomplish all these things by managing its customer database and by offering value-added services that their competitors do not offer. Is Hal Com less expensive than their competitors? I don't know; Hal Com is so good that I don't do comparison shopping. First-time shopping is often very price sensitive, but repeat business often is not.

Here's an example of surprising service. Our gift certificates are beautiful, elaborate, and expensive, and we sell many of them. To keep the price down, we order them in quantities of 2,000. In September we got a call from Mort Caine, of Executive Printing, the firm that prints them. He wanted to know how we were stocked on our gift certificates. Mort said, "I know the holidays are coming and how important it is for you not to run out of gift certificates at that time. I wanted to remind you that it usually takes at least 3 weeks to print and deliver an order." Mort also asked us to check the stock on our menu of services, which also takes 3 weeks to print and are used a lot during the holidays. When we checked, we realized we didn't have enough gift certificates or menus to get us through the holidays.

Mort's phone call was an extremely profitable one for Executive Printing. Some people might think it's pushy for a company to call its clients in this way, but Executive Printing did me a favor by making it a point to know my business and help us avoid getting caught asleep at the wheel. If he hadn't called, we wouldn't have realized we were out of gift certificates and menus until early December, when it would have been too late to reorder them for the most important and busiest time of the year. We would have had egg on our face, not exactly the image we want to project.

## Under-Promise and Over-Deliver

Many car dealerships provide you with a loaner car of the same value as the car you are having repaired. That's a useful service, but here's one better. A friend of mine took his Lexus to Classic Lexus in Mentor, Ohio, for an oil change and couldn't wait while it was being done. The service wasn't covered by warranty, but Classic gave him an upgrade, a new LS 430, to drive that day. When Classic Lexus called to tell him that his car was ready, he told them to keep it because he wanted to trade it in for the LS 430 Lexus he was driving. That's Secret Service at work. It pays to be overly generous.

Metro Lexus of Brookpark, Ohio, won't be outdone. A customer who has purchased a Lexus there can bring his car in every Saturday for a free wash. When a customer needs service, Metro will drop off a loaner car and pick up the customer's Lexus within a 2-hour radius of their dealership, so the customer never has to come to them. This service has been instrumental in attracting customers from near and far.

Saturn has night and weekend hours for service; provides customers with shuttle service while their car is in for maintenance; or, if a dealership is across the street from a movie theater, may provide a ticket to the movies while the car is being fixed. Saturn also has a 30-day money-back guarantee policy; the customer can return the car within 30 days for any reason, even if he or she no longer likes the color. Every year Saturn holds a customer appreciation day at such a destination as Sea World. For its people, Saturn holds weekly management meetings where people get up and say who has been a hero; it could be someone who weeds the flowerbeds or who drove 50 miles to replace a customer's lost key.

### GOING ABOVE AND BEYOND

One afternoon a man called the salon to inquire about our spa packages. Denise Thompson, a receptionist at the time, gave him all the details of all the packages: what they included, the prices, and even her favorites.

"How late are you open?" the man asked Denise.

"Until 8:00 P.M., but I can mail it to you or the recipient to save you the trip."

"No, I have to pick it up today. It's a gift for my wife, and our anniversary is today."

"Great. I'll have it all ready by the time you get here."

At 7:45 P.M., the phone rang and Denise answered. It was the man again.

"Hello. I called earlier about getting my wife a gift certificate. I got stuck at work and there's no way I am going to make it there by 8:00, but thanks anyway."

"I have to balance my drawer and close up. I usually don't get out of here until 8:30 or 8:45, so if you still want to come, I will be here until then."

"Are you kidding? That's awesome. My wife is already angry because I'm working late on our anniversary. It would be great if I could bring her this gift tonight."

Just as Denise was finishing up, the phone rang. It was the man again.

"Denise, you have been so helpful, but I'm afraid I have run out of time. I'm in my car and I have at least 20 more minutes on the freeway before I can get there. I am so sorry if I have inconvenienced you at all. I shouldn't have waited until the last minute to take care of this. I just hope my wife understands."

"Where do you live?"

"In South Euclid."

"I drive through South Euclid on my way home. Do you want me to meet you with the gift certificate?"

"I can't ask you to do that."

"It's not a problem. I just need directions."

"How can I ever thank you?"

"It's my pleasure. Besides it's part of my job."

The next day the man called me.

"Mr. DiJulius, I have to tell you something that happened yesterday with one of your managers."

At first I cringed, thinking, "Oh no, what did we do?" When he told me the story, I felt so proud. I thanked him and said that Denise was not a manager; she had only been with us 6 months, and she was a receptionist, but obviously a good one. He was even more amazed that someone who was not the owner or a manager had behaved in this way.

I immediately called Denise and congratulated her for going above and beyond her duty for one of our guests.

"Denise, why is he under the impression that South Euclid was on your way home? You live in the opposite direction."

"I'm sorry for not telling the truth, but I'm sure he would never have agreed to meet me if he knew that."

### Creating Secret Service

- Recognize all your existing Secret Service systems you already have in place.
- Analyze every point of a customer's encounter and determine the ideal experience that customer would have. Include and enroll your staff's involvement so they have buy in.
- Create a wish list of new Secret Service systems that you would ideally love to execute on a consistent basis.
- From these three lists, create the customer service cycle.
- Start adding to this Customer Experience Cycle from brainstorming groups, new input, and your experiences with other companies and industries that you now recognize as a Secret Service system.
- Have distinguished systems for new and returning customers, from start to finish.
- Create follow-up and customer recovery systems as well.
- Most importantly you need to create the awareness campaign that sells Secret Service to your entire organization so they understand the significance. How it impacts the bottom line, the points of difference, and its benefits.
- Once you have a strong Customer Experience Cycle established, you must now create and revise all your training to include this as an integral part, from orientation on.
- No employee should be allowed to interact with any customer until he or she passes certification—tests, role playing, and so forth that assures you he or she understands every step of your Secret Service

systems and knows the importance of executing it 100 percent of the time.

■ Create checks and balances to ensure it's being done consistently. For example, use secret shoppers or survey customers.

■ Celebrate successes, letters from satisfied customers, and track their impact. Among things you can celebrate are an increase in referrals, retention rates, average number of tickets sold, and examples when employees go above and beyond.

# CHAPTER 2

# Secret Service at Work:

## Implementing Secret Service Systems

A great example of implementing Secret Service is what I call "mastering the Norm factor." I took this from the popular sitcom "Cheers," based on a bar in the Boston area, whose theme song ran, "Where everyone knows your name, and they're always glad you came." Whenever Norm, a popular regular, walked into Cheers, everyone yelled, "Norrrm." He had his own stool at the end of the bar and a permanent bar tab. The bartenders, barmaids, and customers all knew Norm and were familiar with his personal life.

What would happen if Norm walked into Cheers and found a new bartender who didn't know him? What if no one recognized or acknowledged him? Would Norm make Cheers the only bar he frequented or go there as often as he did? Probably not. It's safe to say that Norm would not be as good a customer if he weren't made to feel special.

The more people you make feel like Norm, the more successful your business will be.

That is Secret Service: making clients feel special, like regulars, by remembering their names, preferences, and personal things about them. How often is regular? The term is relative. The best companies make a client feel like a regular even if he comes in only twice a year.

31

TGI Fridays Corporation alludes to Norm in what they call the corner-bar theory in their bartender-training manuals: Make everyone feel like a welcome guest in your home, greet everyone by name and shake hands, and go above and beyond to make all customers feel welcome.

Think about your favorite restaurant, hardware store, grocery store, or coffee shop. Why do you really like to go there? In most cases, you feel the way Norm did. When you want to impress someone, where do you take him to dinner? You go to the place that treats you special, making you feel like a VIP.

I'll admit that I love walking into places and being asked, "How are your sons Johnni, Cal, and Bo doing? How's business?" I tend to trust these more and listen to their people's advice more. And I spend a great deal more money at these places than anywhere else.

Now think of where you don't feel special, and are left feeling frustrated. It's easy to see how much more business and loyalty you probably would have given all of these businesses if they had given you more attention and recognition.

The better the service, the less price becomes an issue.

John Robert's built its entire business by utilizing Secret Service systems. We started small, but soon the number of employees grew from 6 to 20 to 45 to more than 100. The clientele grew from 500 to 10,000 to more than 30,000. As the clientele, staff, and space all grew, we realized that we had to develop training programs to ensure that all employees utilized the Secret Service systems we created to provide a memorable experience. We put dozens of systems in place to increase the chances of exceeding our customer expectations.

I knew we were succeeding when a customer told us about a conversation with her husband, who was looking at their checkbook to decide what expenses they could reduce or eliminate.

"One of the things we can reduce or eliminate is John Robert's," he said.

"Don't even think about that. I will pack my lunch, give up our vacation, or stop eating out. I'll even quit smoking. But John Robert's is a non-negotiable. It's up there with food, rent, and utilities."

Since hearing that, we have made non-negotiable customer service our theme. We constantly ask each other, "Are you delivering non-negotiable service?"

Of all the businesses you use on a regular basis, do even 5 percent of them deliver truly legendary customer service? I expect not. Is it any wonder that nine out of out ten companies go out of business within the first 5 years? But I have rarely heard of a company with exceptional customer service going out of business. Show me a company with great customer service, and I will show you one that is well run, at the top of its industry.

A deeply ingrained myth in our society is that the best companies are the best because they hire only the best people. So companies that want to become the best try to do it by raising their hiring standards. I think the truth is quite different, that less than 10 percent of the population knows what outstanding customer service is and can deliver it on the day they are hired.

The best companies know there aren't enough of the best people out there, so they hire good people with the potential to deliver exceptional customer service; then, through an awareness campaign, in training that starts on day one, and attention every day thereafter, the best companies turn those good people into the best.

## Personalize the Service

As the corporate elephants are discovering, they need to create Secret Service systems to be able to deliver that personalized service that mom-and-pop shops can deliver.

When I was building my client base, I learned a useful technique that helped me deliver a more personalized experience, and I have since incorporated it into our training program. Although I have a good memory, it sometimes takes three or four visits before I can remember a client well. To be able to recall exactly who each client is, I began keeping notes on my clients in our computer.

The database jogged my memory of exactly who this client was, and then the rest would come back to me. On the rare occasions when I did need to rely on my notes, this technique ensured that the client got the same great experience that any other regular would receive.

When I was notified that my next client had arrived, I looked on the computer screen, and if I didn't recognize her name, I accessed the software information about customer preferences, which tells us virtually everything. If the appointment was highlighted in green, that meant the client was a return request, someone who had been to me previously and had requested me again. Sometimes my appointment was a return request but I didn't remember her. I didn't want to walk into the check-in area, see 10 clients waiting, and look around blankly and say her name as if I didn't have a clue who she was.

I'd send my assistant to the check-in area to greet my client and escort her to my station for a consultation. In the meantime, I looked up the notes that I enter after each visit. I may have seen this client a few times, but a busy hairdresser with several hundred clients can't remember them all. The information in the computer told me the last time she was in, what service she had done, what products she purchased in the past, if she has referred anyone, and any other personal information I entered.

Having done my research, when I consulted with the client I could say "Alice. How are you? Tell me, did you like the highlights we did last time? Thank you so much for referring your friend, Margaret. Did you receive your $5 gift certificate for referring her? How was your trip to the Bahamas with your fiancé?"

During the haircut, since I am aware of what hair products she has purchased and when, I could recommend products based on what she has bought, how long ago, and what else she might use. If I saw that she hasn't purchased conditioner for 6 or 7 months, I could say, "Alice, how is that Rosemary Mint Conditioner? Are you running low yet?" Or if I saw that she has purchased shampoo, conditioner, and gel but has never purchased hair spray, I could tell her how great our hair spray is and which one works best with her type of hair.

This technique is so simple and takes only seconds of my time, but, besides helping me remember all clients, it gives me a powerful way to impress clients and make them feel like they're my only client. Because they feel so special, they continue to come back again and again, and they refer their family and friends to us.

## Take the Initiative

In Shep Hyken's excellent book *The Loyal Customer*, he explains how a cab driver does little things to make a simple cab ride a memorable experience. When you enter his cab, the first thing you notice is that it's spotless, something you cannot take for granted. Next, in the back seat you notice a cooler stocked with juices, water, and soda. Chips and crackers are available, as well as a local paper, *The Wall Street Journal*, and *USA Today*.

He offers all these things free of charge. How much could it cost if a passenger drinks a bottle of soda, reads a newspaper, and has a bag of crackers? Maybe $1.50, if the driver bought them in bulk. Don't you think he makes up that $1.50 and much more in tips and return fares?

At the end of the ride, this cab driver gets your business card and mails you a thank you note saying how much he appreciated your business and inviting you to contact him if you're in the area again. Because of this exemplary customer service, he is booked with repeat fares all day. He doesn't have to wait in a line for 20 minutes at the airport with all the other cab drivers.

## *Hyde Park Grille*

Hyde Park Grille, in Moreland Hills, Ohio, does an outstanding job of using Secret Service systems. A lot of millionaires, sports figures, and local celebrities dine here regularly. The biggest reason for Hyde Park's success is its general manager, Robert Hughes, who truly understands customer service. Everyone who works for him is a product of his training and also gives fine service.

Stacy and I have always enjoyed the food at Hyde Park, but that alone does not justify how often we go there and the amount of money we spend. Whenever I take guests to Hyde Park, they think I am a celebrity. Many staff members stop at our table to say, "Hello, Mr. and Mrs. DiJulius. How are the salons doing?" Then they add something personal, like, "My best friend goes to your Mayfield spa and raves about it."

Here's how Hyde Park Grille utilizes a system like John Robert's white cape system. The kitchen area posts a diagram that all servers and staff refer to. It shows all the tables, and each table is classified in one of four categories: new customer, regular, tuxedo, or spotlight. Robert Hughes defines a regular as a returning customer who enjoys the meal and the service but doesn't like a lot of extra attention. A tuxedo is a customer who, like me, enjoys all the great attention and fuss. For a tuxedo, the staff makes sure that a few people stop at that table and acknowledge the customer. Finally, a spotlight is someone in any of the other three categories who is having a VIP dinner, such as entertaining an important client or out-of-town guest. How does the staff identify a VIP? It's simple. When you call to make a reservation, you are asked, "Is it a special occasion?" Before every shift, Hyde Park has a meeting during which they go over this information. It can have a huge impact on their customer's experience.

By no means do Stacy and I stand out among the millionaires and celebrities who frequent Hyde Park Grille, but we and our guests are always made to feel as if we do. The restaurant has hundreds of regular customers who spend more money than Stacy and I, but you would never know it. Remember that a regular may come in weekly, monthly, or annually.

## The Perfect Restaurant Experience
Whatever the mind can conceive and believe, the mind can achieve.
—Napoleon Hill

Despite Hyde Park Grille's excellent secret service, I have yet to see a restaurant master the total experience. Here is my vision of the perfect experience at a restaurant I'll call Dante's. Let's assume that Stacy and I have been there before, and we're bringing friends who have never been to Dante's. When we arrive, the valet greets us and asks our name but does not give us a claim ticket. As we walk in, the maitre d' welcomes us by name. He takes our coats; again we receive no claim ticket.

A hostess greets us by name and escorts us to our table. The busboy comes to our table with water, looks at Stacy and me and says, "Welcome back, Mr. and Mrs. DiJulius. It's great to see you again." He then says to our friends, "I would like to welcome you, Mr. and Mrs. Pannitto. You are in for a wonderful experience. My name is James, and my team and I are here to make sure all of you have an exceptionally good time this evening. The team serving you tonight is Susan, your waitress; Tom, your wine steward; and myself. Please do not hesitate to ask us for anything that will make your evening more enjoyable."

Susan arrives and greets us in similar style. She says, "Mrs. DiJulius, would you like a glass of the Magnificot wine you enjoy, or would you like a bottle for the table? Mr. DiJulius, can I get you started with a Seven & Seven?" When we pick up our menus, printed daily with the date and the day's specials, we notice that one special is the DiJulius appetizer.

The whole evening goes this way. Everyone who comes to our table greets us by name, welcomes us back, knows it's the Pannittos' first visit, and gives them a detailed explanation of what to expect and how menu items are prepared. After dinner, we get a dessert menu, and one item is the "Pannitto soufflé."

After the meal we head toward the door, where the maitre d' has our coats ready for us. He asks how everything was, tells us it was a pleasure having us, and says he hopes to see us again soon. When we walk outside, our car is waiting, warmed up and ready to go. What an evening. What an experience.

Is that restaurant experience possible? Is it cost-effective to pull off? If that really happened, would the place be packed? Yes, yes, and yes. Nearly everything that happened in this perfect scenario costs almost nothing extra to execute.

First, when we call to make reservations, we are asked not only for our names but also the names of everyone in our party. On the day of our reservation, when the day's menu is printed, the guest list is used, producing a DiJulius appetizer and a Pannitto dessert.

We don't need a claim ticket for our car or coats because when we give the valet our name, he keeps track of our automobile by name instead of by number, and he uses the intercom to tell the maitre d' that the DiJulius party is on the way in.

When we are seated, our party is entered into the software system, which shows our table, that we are returning customers (coded in green), and that our guests (in blue) are first-timers. Everyone who comes to our table quickly reviews the information on the computer to personalize the contact. Before the waitress comes to our table, she reviews our history to see what we traditionally order; when she presents our bill, she tells the coat check and valet that we will be leaving soon, so our coats and car are waiting for us.

It's that simple. Hardly any extra work or expense is involved in executing Secret Service. Most high-end restaurants already have a good software system and print daily menus, so custom menus, one page for each customer, can be printed easily and cost pennies; software will print the menu from the reservation list, similar to a mail merge.

If and when it opens, this will be the most sought-after restaurant in the area. It can charge premium prices. Its highly trained staff of waiters, busboys, valets, and coat-room attendants would make 20 to 50 percent more than those at any other restaurant in a 50-mile radius.

## Golf Courses

Fowler's Mill Golf Course in Chesterland, Ohio, has its version of the white cape system. Group outings constitute a significant part of their business, so it's critical that groups return on an annual basis. Each group's leader and decision-maker has a Tournament Director pin on his shirt so that the entire staff knows who he is and can be sure to treat him like a VIP wherever he goes at Fowler's Mill.

If, for example, this person is standing in a long line at the snack counter, the employee makes sure he is taken care of immediately, saying "I know you really don't have time to wait here. You need to get back with your party, so tell me what you need and I will bring it to you and put it on your bill." Or, a golf cart, no matter how scarce it may be, is always available, no questions asked, for someone wearing a tournament director's pin. Do you think that person will decide to bring his group again next year?

## Nordstrom's

Nordstrom's, documented often for its superior customer service, has a concierge who provides umbrellas, wheelchairs, strollers, and checking service for coats and packages. The concierge can also send a fax, issue gift certificates, offer sightseeing suggestions, call cabs, and make restaurant or theater reservations. Diaper-changing areas are located in all lounges, in the men's as well as women's, and family restrooms enable either parent to take a child to the bathroom. Shoeshine service is available. A Nordstrom's in Illinois even donated space for a mammography center operated by local hospitals; women can shop until paged for their appointment.

## Ritz Carlton

The Ritz Carlton Hotel has also been documented often for exemplary customer service. Whoever is the first employee to come across a customer complaint owns that complaint and is personally responsible for handling it. The Ritz has mastered its own set of Secret Service systems. If you stay at one location and tell them you need a specific type of pillow, you will get it, and the next time you stay at a Ritz Carlton Hotel anywhere, that type of pillow is likely to be waiting for you.

Stacy and I had our own Ritz experience in Cleveland while attending a wedding. The shoulder strap on Stacy's dress broke. A waitress noticed her dilemma, discreetly told Stacy to follow her, and found someone to come to the ladies' room and sew Stacy's strap back on. In 15 minutes Stacy was back at our table, her dress like new.

How does the Ritz do this type of thing constantly, at every location? A tear in a dress is not something they can anticipate, yet there was an employee who stepped up and handled it without being instructed to do so by a superior. The answer is training and managed systems. Customers have had similar dilemmas in the past, so they were prepared to handle it.

The Ritz is also a role model for inputting and managing guest preferences. Their outstanding training ensures their staff will carry on the Ritz legacy and go above and beyond for their customers. For example, they have a 21-day retraining orientation. They quiz new hires and have them go on a scavenger hunt where they find out the answers to many questions about the property. They also have an "in-line" meeting each morning where they go over the "basics" and the credo. The Ritz has information printed for the employees that gives them any guest challenges from the previous day, employee news (birthdays, etc.), information on each of the guests (who is returning, who stayed at another Ritz property, what their preferences are, etc.). Information on customer preferences comes from all members of the team. For example, a housekeeper could see by what is left in the trash receptacle that the customer likes Coke, or prefers foam pillows. The Ritz creates airtight systems and training for its employees to enter these kinds of preferences in their database and utilize it to customize each guest's experience.

## Hertz

Rental car companies have turned around their procedures and have made life so much easier. Returning a rental car to an airport used to be a nightmare; now you simply pull into the parking lot, and an employee greets you and gives you a receipt printed from a hand-held computer. What could be better and more efficient? Hertz Club Gold has taken this one step further. Hertz's program allows you to have a car waiting for you without the hassle of waiting in lines or signing rental agreements. When you get off the plane and enter the terminal, you see your name in lights on a sign that tells you where your rental car is waiting; you drive it to the exit gate, show your license, and drive away. What could be easier? The beauty of this procedure is that you don't need to have premier status or earn so many points or be a frequent renter. Anyone can sign up for and receive premier treatment.

## Wal-Mart

Mass merchandising is one of the hardest businesses in which to deliver unforgettable customer service, but it's not impossible. These companies are so big that most of their face-to-face interaction with customers does not allow them to utilize an information database until the customer is at the checkout counter; by then it's too late. Despite the challenge, mass merchants can still deliver great customer service. The best of the best develop systems for their associates so they can better interact with their customers, mostly in the store aisles.

Wal-Mart is known for two distinctive Secret Service systems they implement at all their locations. The first is the Wal-Mart greeter, a concept copied by nearly every mass merchant. A cheerful person greets you at the door and is available immediately to direct you to the right aisle or answer a question about something the store may carry. The second one is just as powerful that we have tried to emulate. Whenever Wal-Mart employees come within 10 feet of a customer, they greet the customer. Not only does this help make customers feel more at home, it also makes them feel more comfortable about asking the greeting employee questions, which can only result in better service and higher sales.

Another way mass merchants try to provide better customer service is by localizing their product mix. For example, a Wal-Mart executive realized that a store in a predominantly ethnic community had only a few rows of ethnic products and that a store in a predominantly rental community had a huge display of snow-blowers. By looking at the demographics of each area, Wal-Mart is better able to localize the merchandise and increase sales.

## Joann Fabrics

Joann Fabrics and Crafts, the nationwide leader in its field, works to achieve superior service by having every team member ask the customer one simple question, "What are you making?" People who shop at Joann Fabrics and Crafts are there because they are making something, be it clothes, a holiday wreath, or a merchandising display. Asking "What are you making?" does two things. First, it personalizes the visit: Customers love to talk about what they are doing, and they feel good that employees care. Second, the question creates an opportunity for additional sales; the team member can ensure this customer has thought of everything and can advise her on additional products the customer may not have thought of. This approach is especially effective because instead of trying to roll out a million different concepts, it has kept it simple.

## Landlords

All businesses have the potential to exceed customer expectations. Consider landlords. Their customers are called tenants. On a tenant's anniversary, for example, the landlord could say, "Would you like a new ceiling fan or a new garbage disposal?" Maybe the tenant could have a $200 allowance. The landlord who does that would have a very low vacancy rate. Landlords can even offer referral incentives to tenants, some type of discount off their rent when they refer a new tenant. It would be worth the money when you consider how much more a landlord pays a real estate broker who does the same thing.

## Go Above and Beyond

One of my favorite hotels is the Hilton. We hold many functions at the Hilton in Beachwood, Ohio, every year mainly because it gives us such outstanding service. Talk about exceeding one's expectations. One of the functions we hold there is our Johnni's, a black-tie event for all our employees. We present many awards; winners are surprised, and they make speeches.

At the Johnni's in 2000, we discovered that Linda Gorski, an employee who was to receive an Employee of the Year Award, had a terrible case of flu and was absent. We knew how hard Linda had worked and that she wouldn't want to miss it, so we called her and said that her daughter Kelly, who also worked for us, had won a big award. Could Linda possibly come at 9:00 P.M., when we would present the award? Linda said yes, but she couldn't drive, so we promised to send someone to pick her up. Because the event had already started, we couldn't ask anyone from John Robert's to go. At 8 P.M. I asked Andria Katz, the general manager of the Hilton, if she could have a limousine service bring Linda, and Andria said she would take care of it. Without fail, Linda arrived just before 9:00 P.M., and to her surprise, she was the winner and was able to accept her award.

As I was checking out of the Hilton, I asked how much I owed for the limousine and was told there was no charge. I said, "Nonsense. I appreciate getting limousine service on such short notice, and I want to pay for it." The assistant manager explained that it was impossible to get a limousine on such short notice. I asked who picked up Linda. It was Andria Katz. In addition, that evening she had also personally run up to my room for my car keys, gone to my car for my video camera, delivered it to me in the ballroom, returned my car keys to my room, and returned my room key to me.

What impressed me most of all was the fact that the employees didn't make me aware of it. This was truly Secret Service. Ms. Katz wanted our event to run smoothly, and she made a point of not letting me know she was the one who had done all this. She provided services that many general managers would consider beneath them.

It's no wonder I received such above and beyond service. As part of their training, employees take customer service courses on sales and service that includes deals with customers and relationship building. Training is done at the hotel corporate level and in-house. First managers attend, then staff. Continuous training is provided, and one of the most important policies that they repeat is empowerment training, which is allowing any employee to "handle" a situation without needing or fearing management approval.

A Secret Service system for going above and beyond is probably the hardest thing for any business to institute. It may not be possible to ensure that everyone in the organization does this, but when the leader in the organization continuously displays outstanding customer service, it's certain to trickle down to the rest of the staff. Consider these examples from John Roberts:

- It's not unusual for our employees to make special trips to clients who can't get to us. Christine McCreight, a hairdresser, excels at exceeding our clients' expectations. For example, during a trial hair-and-makeup session for a client about to get married, the bride-to-be mentioned that she did not have a purse to go with her wedding dress and would have to do without. When she came to John Robert's the day of her wedding to have her hair done, she was amazed when Christine presented her with a gift. It was a purse that matched her wedding dress and was filled with aspirin, hair products, needle and thread, pins, and breath mints.
- Loss of water or electricity in an emergency has closed many a salon. Our employees have been creative in finding ways around such obstacles. One day we had no water, which we need for shampoos, color jobs, permanents, and pedicures. After some quick thinking, guest care employee Corey Rothman sent staff out to purchase five gallons of bottled water. We heated the water in our microwave, and it held us over until the water was turned back on.

One day we lost electricity for several hours. We had to cancel all appointments, but one client urgently needed her hair done for a big event that night. One of our hairdressers, Nick Montecalvo, lived nearby and volunteered to take this client to his house and do her hair there.

- One of our clients made an appointment to get her hair styled and her nails done the day she was to receive an important award. On the big day she called us in tears because she was snowed in and couldn't get out of her driveway. One of our managers, Eric Hammond, volunteered to go to her house, pick her up, bring her to the salon, and drive her home.

- A client was in our spa the day before her son's wedding and mentioned to Lisa Adams that the dry cleaner had ruined the blouse she was going to wear. The client was very frustrated and was contemplating canceling the rest of her spa services to shop for another blouse. During her facial she had described its color and style, so afterward, without saying anything to the client, Lisa began to call every boutique and department store. She guessed the size, and when she located the perfect blouse, she put it on hold under the client's name. Returning to the spa lounge, Lisa told the client, who was thrilled. With permission, using the client's credit card, Lisa made the purchase by phone. The client could relax and finish the rest of her spa day.

- During a pedicure, an elderly client remarked that she had to go home and finish packing because she was moving, but she didn't know how she was going to do it alone. Edie Bennett, her nail technician, borrowed her husband's truck after work and helped the client move.

- One of our facialists, Lindsay Boros, regularly goes above and beyond for her clients. She brings the client's car to the door so the client won't ruin her hairdo, makeup, and nails. She runs grocery errands for clients. If she overhears a client mention a craving for a glazed doughnut or pizza or deli item, she runs out to get it and has it waiting when the client leaves the spa. If it's a client's birthday, she arranges to have balloons and cake waiting. She has taken a client to the hospital and stayed with her until a family member arrived. Lindsay does not regard any of this as special. "I do this sort of stuff every day. It's part of our job to make a client's day. This should not be considered going above and beyond. It should be thought of as routine."

## Be Ethical and Decent

Concentrate not on making a lot of money, but on becoming the type of person people want to do business with.

—*Patricia Fripp*

High Noon Restaurant of Battle Creek, Michigan, has you fill out a card when you first visit and then they have all your information in their software. When you call for a future reservation they give you a reservation code. You can reserve on line by going to opentable.com and reserve your seat.

They keep a client history on you so they know when special occasions are. They are known for greeting their customers by name. If they can, they direct customers to the bar where the bartender has their drinks already mixed. They send information via the Internet on upcoming wine dinners, chef's table events, cooking classes, and so forth. They have contests that customers can enter to win a chef's table, and so forth. All these communications are sent using the Internet. When customers attend their Wine Dinner, they pass a menu around to have all of the guests sign it, then frame it and hang it in the restaurant. These special communications and techniques make guests feel like celebrities.

I have the greatest remodeler-carpenter-handyman in the world. He is Brian Hooper, owner of Hooper Homes, in Bainbridge, Ohio. Brian doesn't attend any business seminars or read many business books on how to do it better. Most of what Brian does well happens because he is a decent person. I could fill this chapter with all the little things Brian does for his customers on a day-to-day basis. In ten years I have used Hooper Homes hundreds of times, at John Robert's and at home, and I have referred Hooper Homes to hundreds of people. Not once have I heard of anyone who had a less-than-excellent experience.

First, Brian is one of the most dependable people I have ever met. If he says he will do something, it is like money in the bank. It's done the way he promised and by the time he promised. His level of honesty and integrity is rare in any business, let alone the construction business.

He routinely responds to emergencies on the weekend as well as performs all kinds of little extras. For example, once he saw the lady of the house struggling to put some bicycles in her van so she could go put air in the tires. Brian had one of his workers put the bikes in his truck and run them up to the gas station to fill the tires for the lady. It's obvious why there is such a demand for his services and why people will wait two or three months for him.

Brian will never promise something that he knows he can't deliver, just to get a job. Often he tells someone up front that it will be six to eight weeks before he can start on a project, and because of his reputation, people usually wait.

Brian and I brainstormed on how he can take his business to the next level, and he implemented a number of systems used by John Robert's. Brian started sending out thank you cards to new clients and to everyone who referred a client to him. When he meets someone at a party who mentions wanting some work done, he sends a note saying, "It was a pleasure to meet you, and if you ever need me for anything, please call." After he completes a big job, he often sends a thank you card with a gift certificate (to John Robert's, of course). It takes Brian just 10 minutes once a week to manage this system. Every Sunday he reviews the past week to identify the jobs that are new or that came from referrals, and he sends out thank you postcards. This system does not take much time, but it produces an enormous amount of good will.

## New York Life Insurance
People don't care how much you know until they know how much you care.

Larry Gould is a life insurance advisor for New York Life. I met him after our daily newspaper ran a long story about John Robert's, including a picture of Stacy and me, on the front page of the business section.

This kind of exposure is great, but it also means that every salesman within 50 miles calls us, stops in, and sends letters.

Larry walked into our corporate offices a few days later with a gift for us. Nobody had ever seen him before. He said he saw the article in the paper and, to congratulate us, presented us with the article bronzed on a plaque, beautiful and obviously very expensive.

Immediately suspicious, I asked, "What's your pitch?"

He said, "Nothing, I just want to congratulate you. I love to see young people succeed."

We started talking about different things, and Larry seemed to know something about everything. When we told him we were going to New York City, he told us the best restaurants to go to, and we discovered he was right.

Larry started coming in once a month for a haircut, even though he obviously didn't need it. I always looked forward to his next visit because he knows so much about so many things—business, family, people—you name a topic and he knows about it. One day he said, "Someday when you're not too busy, I would love to sit down with you and explain some ways that I could help you save money and take care of your family through some vehicles I can provide, such as life insurance, estate planning, and so on."

I had already heard that same line from dozens of people selling life insurance, but never from someone who had given me so much first. Larry knows the secret to making people want to do business with him. He talks about what interests them and about how to help them get what they want. He doesn't spend any time talking about what interests him or what he wants. Eventually I bought a small term-life policy because I needed it and because I wanted to give Larry the business. He had more than earned it.

Larry's service didn't stop there. Next he asked when would be a good day to come to our house and meet our boys. I said Saturdays were good, and the next Saturday Larry stopped by, met the boys, and had presents for them. About a year later, he asked if he and his wife could take my family to dinner. He took us to an outstanding Chinese restaurant with unbelievable service. I should have expected that Larry would deal only with the very best.

About this time, Larry started to drop off a loaf of bread every Friday for every employee at our salons. When I asked him the reason, he said that as long as he could remember, he had been doing this for his best customers. In no way was I one of his best customers. Up to this point, all I had purchased was a small term-life policy.

Larry just turned 75. What's the secret of his success? He says, "If you have a client who needs a job, then help him with a resume and introduce him to your contacts. If you know someone who is looking for funds, then introduce him to potential investors. If you know someone who is looking for an employee, then help him find a key person. If you know someone who is looking for a loan, then fix him up with a banker. Be a resource for people. Learn to help people first, long before you ever ask for the sale." This approach has me constantly thinking, How can I give him more of my business?

## Proflowers.com

When you place an order with Proflowers.com, they manage and communicate every step of the entire process. As soon as you have placed your order online, you immediately get an e-mail confirmation that they received your order and are processing it. When your order leaves their building, they send you an e-mail notification that includes a tracking number. Finally, they send an e-mail when your order has been delivered, along with the name of the person who signed for it.

Proflowers.com is also an extremely proactive company. Two months before Valentine's Day, to prepare customers for price increases and reduce complaints, Proflowers.com sends an e-mail to alert customers to a coming price increase in January—and to give them the opportunity to place their Valentine's Day order before the price goes up. Proflowers.com has annual sales of $27 million, and most of those sales are transacted online without phone assistance. With so many more consumers shopping online now, one of the biggest difficulties is trying to provide personalized customer service over the web. Proflowers.com has tackled that challenge head on.

## Amazon.com

Repeat customers accounted for 71% of Amazon's sales in 1999. Amazon acquires the necessary information to know who their customers are and their preferences. It then uses this knowledge to offer value-added features to its customers, such as 1-Click, Wish List, and recommendations to create a personalized and convenient experience that results in repeat purchases.

If you log onto Amazon.com to purchase a book—let's say you want to buy *Secret Service* for a business associate—Amazon would provide you with the book's rank among books purchased through Amazon, the book's average customer rating, reviews about the book, as well as recommendations of several other titles with similar subject matter. Then the site encourages you to rate the book as well as the reviews on the book. This helps provide a dual tie-in, the customer receives useful suggestions from other customers, as well as provides his or her advice to others, creating a network with other Amazon readers.

The Wish List does something similar. Customers have the ability to create an online "family and friends" group that can share gift lists and recommendations on books, CDs, and so forth. Amazon customers can search for the Wish Lists of people they know and make their buying selection based on that, choosing a gift that will be appreciated.

Amazon also understands the importance of providing real life human encounter. You can contact them live, 24 hours a day, toll free or via e-mail if you wish. Once your order is placed, you receive a thank you confirmation e-mail, including order number, delivery date, additional recommendations, and a link to track the order. If you order multiple items, Amazon will immediately e-mail the customer, giving him the option to have the order held until it's all in or have the available items sent now.

Amazon.com, doing business in a world that exists over the Internet, is providing better personalized service than many companies that have the benefit of face-to-face interaction with their customers on daily basis. With this kind of service, is there any question why they are a leader in repeat business?

## UPS

UPS now offers its customers the option of being notified when a package will arrive. Now you can know precisely when a shipment will arrive, and if it's C.O.D., you can have the money ready for a UPS driver, reducing his wait time.

## Famous Supply

How important is 24-hour emergency service to your customers? Famous Supply is a distributor of HVAC, plumbing, and building products in Pennsylvania, western Virginia, and Ohio. This company now offers 24-hour emergency service at many of its locations. For example, if any repairman needs a part to fix someone's furnace on a Saturday night in the dead of winter, he contacts Famous Supply's 24-hour emergency service, which delivers the part right away. The family doesn't have to go to a hotel for the weekend or run the risk of their pipes freezing. This is double Secret Service because Famous Supply delivers excellent service and does it behind the scenes, enabling the repairman to deliver outstanding service to his customers when they really need it.

## Bob's Automotive

On the philosophy of "Honest repairs for honest people," Bob's Automotive has built an incredibly successful business in Fairfield, Iowa, population 10,000. Bob's Automotive does two things that stand out and that many businesses could replicate. First, when you drop your car off at Bob's, you receive an estimate within one hour. Second, the actual bill is always less than the estimate. Think about it: the mechanic quotes you an estimate of $350 and you tell him to go ahead. When you arrive at the cashier's window, your bill says $315. That's Secret Service. Some owners might be reluctant to do this because it might be perceived as overbidding and undercharging. But if you consistently deliver a great product or service, most people don't price-check businesses they trust.

## Banks

In recent years banks have been providing many new services that make it so much more convenient for the customer. Thanks to computer technology, I personally have not set foot in a bank in more than three years. I have direct deposit, and I now pay my bills, view my accounts, and transfer funds entirely online. When I need to see my banker, for something like a car or business loan or a new account, my banker comes to me.

U.S. Bank, headquartered in Minneapolis, is a good example of a bank that is putting its money where its mouth is, so to speak. U.S. Bank has a five-star service guarantee. If U.S. Bank fails to meet any of its guarantees, the customer will receive money back. For instance, the commercial banking group promises to respond the same day to a customer inquiry made before 3:00 P.M. U.S. Bank will respond to a credit request within two business days of receipt. If U.S. Bank falls short on any of its five points, your account will be credited. If you wait in line longer than 5 minutes, you will receive a credit of $5 to your account.

At Keybank, Helen France, a Senior Vice President says, "A bank is a bank, and the only way I can differentiate myself from another banker is through accessibility and constant communications. On my business card I have two e-mail addresses and four phone numbers so I can be reached. My customers know they can call me any time, and they know I mean that. My philosophy is, 'My paycheck may come from the bank, but I work for my client.' "

## Lemonade Stands

Secret Service can be applied to any business, even your child's lemonade stand. What do most children do when they sell lemonade? They make a sign, get a table, make some lemonade, and set up shop on their lawn.

Last summer when he was 9, my son Johnni made $325 in one day selling lemonade. First, he set up his stand at the end of the street (under parental supervision), where every car had to brake for the stop sign. Johnni's sign said, "Super Size Lemonade & Iced Tea to Go." He set things up so that people did not have to make a special stop to buy; they didn't even have to get out of the car. As each car braked for the stop sign, he gestured to the driver and showed him a 16-ounce cup of lemonade or ice tea with a lid on it. Most people rolled down the window, pulled up to the curb, and bought the lemonade to go.

Next Johnni took the lemonade stand mobile. In the mid-afternoon he and his friends went to a new-home construction site in our neighborhood and offered lemonade and iced tea to the dozens of construction workers. Nearly everyone bought something. The twist was that Johnni and his buddies charged a $1 a cup, not the traditional 25 cents. For that dollar, he gave customers a large cup with a lid and delivered it right to them. He and his friends sold more than 300 drinks in about five hours.

This example drives home the point that, "The better the service, the less price becomes an issue." My biggest obstacle now is that he wants to quit school and do this full time.

### Putting Secret Service to work

- Develop a system that distinguishes your "Norms" (VIPs), as well as makes your staff aware of them on every encounter.
- Create a system that helps personalize each customer encounter. Keeping up-to-date personal information on clients in your database that each employee can access.
- Train your staff on how to input and access this information and the benefits of making customers feel like "Norm."
- Brainstorm with your staff on what soft amenities you can provide that would result in an unforgettable experience, for example, soda in a cab ride, free oil refills for jiffy lube in between oil changes, free bang trims at a salon.
- On a daily basis create some type of communication that would enable shifts to know who the customers are for the day, such as preshift meetings, display board in the employee lounge, and so on. Then train your team to use this information to provide personalized service to all your customers, even the ones they are dealing with directly.
- Create a system that distinguishes between new and returning clients that the entire staff can identify and incorporate in their encounter.

# CHAPTER 3

# Your Front Line Is Your Bottom Line:

## The Value of Your Front Line People

Every business begins and ends at the front desk. When people talk about terrible customer service, nine times out of ten it's based on a misstep at the front desk.

Consider your appointment book your bank account. The more you invest in it, the higher your returns will be. It's important therefore to pay attention to and train your front line.

The typical receptionist is like an offensive lineman on a football team. Both have the toughest jobs on their respective teams. The offensive lineman's name is mentioned only once or twice during a game, when the referee tells 80,000 fans and national television audiences, "Number 63 is caught for holding; no first down." Everyone boos Number 63. The referee never mentions the other 99 plays, when the offensive lineman knocked the defensive player down so the quarterback could throw for 300 yards and the running back could score two touchdowns. But it's the names of the quarterback and the running back that appear on the front page of the next day's sports section.

The same scenario plays out in a business. The receptionist is juggling three phone calls, two people checking in, and three people checking out, as well as dealing with complaints. She is scheduling appointments and trying to persuade an irritated client to reschedule after she had been kept waiting an unreasonable length of time. All this goes unnoticed. But if a receptionist double-books an appointment or doesn't allow enough time for it, watch out!

## American Express

Few companies put more emphasis on training their front line people than American Express. Before their telephone service representatives put on a headset, they spend five weeks in a classroom, two weeks in on-the-job training, and another three weeks in a training unit. They learn everything from the company's basic operating policies to the best ways to calm an angry customer, or help a distressed person needing immediate assistance. Their training is a step-by-step process that includes lectures, practice, listening, and role playing. Using information from past experiences, they have developed systems to solve future problems and defuse them before they can escalate any further.

American Express was one of the first credit card companies to provide their customers detailed itemized statements of their credit card usage. It was a great value added, especially to business card members, who, once they had this feature, couldn't do without it, thereby forcing their competition to do the same or lose market share.

## Dedicate Staff to Important Functions

To give the best service to your guests, you need to specialize and departmentalize your front desk team so they can focus totally on the customer.

To give callers the attention they deserve, dedicate a call center to scheduling appointments.

Move your phones away from your front desk. At John Robert's they all ring in a private room staffed by people who are able to take the time to answer questions, present our services well, and explain what particular operator the caller should book and why. We also specialized our check-in and check-out centers. As you walk in, a hostess greets you, takes your coat, pages your operator, and offers you refreshments. If it's your first visit, she also gives you a tour.

With our call center handling all phone calls and the hostess taking care of all the clients checking in, the staff at our check-out desk is now able to ensure that everyone who is leaving has enjoyed her visit, has been given the opportunity to purchase products, and can schedule her next appointment.

## Sell Ad-On Services

Would you like French fries with that?
—McDonald's drive-through teller

The separation of all these tasks has helped our salon and spa give more attention to each client, improve customer service and efficiency, and sell ad-on services. For example, having more time to spend with our callers enabled us to start asking if they would like to book a manicure with their haircuts. Tracking shows that at least 15 out of every 100 clients asked said yes, and that alone pays for the receptionist's day. An even bigger benefit of a private call center is that we have reduced the number of times we put clients on hold from 50 percent to 20 percent. We have also trained our call center personnel, when making confirmation calls for the next day's appointment, to make the guest aware of openings for additional services around the time they plan to come in. Just as when our guests check in, our hostess also informs them of the available appointments we still have on that day.

During the phone call, it's also important before we hang up to ask if there's anything else we can do for the client. We learned this from credit card companies. Whenever I called my credit card company with a question, once I got the information I needed I would thank them and start to hang up and they would always ask "Is there anything else I can do for you today, Mr. DiJulius"? Like many businesses, they have many incoming calls to take and need to be productive with their time. Yet that simple phrase makes a client feel they are willing to take as much time as necessary to take care of him or her, and that the client is their only concern at that moment.

## Answer the Real Question

How a customer service representative answers a question is critical. It's a good idea to arm your guest care department with scripts so they can give better responses to frequently asked questions.

This procedure eliminated a problem at John Robert's: A guest care person would answer our phones, listen for a moment, say, "Between $40 and $100," then say, "Thank you," and hang up. The caller was asking: "How much are your haircuts?" At John Robert's haircuts are about more than just the price.

The correct answer is, "Our haircut prices vary depending on the level of our designers. Our designer levels are based on their experience and amount of advanced education. Each level is a different price, ranging from $40 to $100, and all of them include a stress-relieving treatment, shampoo, hand and arm massage, haircut and style, makeup application, and product consultation. Would you like to schedule a complimentary consultation?"

Once the guest care person knows what day is best for the client, she recommends designers based on their availability and the amount the client wants to spend. The longer the client is on the phone and the more information the guest care associate can share with her, the more likely she is to book an appointment. The client also gets a much clearer understanding of why John Robert's has a range of prices. Before we used this script, callers would initially select a less expensive designer; now many callers select the more experienced and more expensive designers.

It's also important to understand what the caller is really asking you. The people at Disney World say their most frequently asked question is, "What time is the 3 o'clock parade?" Disney has figured out that people are really trying to find out where the good spots are to see the parade, and how early they should arrive. When my family visited Disney, the map of the park said the 3 o'clock parade would take place at 4:00 P.M. that day. The parade is now known as the 3 o'clock parade no matter what time it begins.

Similarly there are many services that are unfamiliar to the new spa consumer. John Robert's gets calls all the time asking, "I have a

60-minute massage at 2:00 P.M. How long will that take?" or, "I am getting a Vichy Shower treatment today. Will I get wet?"

It's important not to give the impression that the caller has asked a silly question. She may be a little self-conscious and nervous about getting a service that requires her to strip down to virtually nothing and trust a stranger. The questions are her way of trying to reduce anxiety. She is really asking, "How long will I be there for a 60-minute massage, and what time should I arrive?" As for the Vichy Shower treatment, the client wants to know what is going to happen or how she should dress.

## Specialization

The same customer service benefits are generated at the check-out desk. Now that we have focused our front desk exclusively on checking people out, we have dramatically increased the number of clients who book their next appointment at the desk. (We have also seen a decrease in billing mistakes because we have time to check the accuracy of the bill; previously, last-minute additional services that clients received often were not put on the bill.)

Consider the impact of prebooking future appointments. Let's say that over a year's time a well-trained front desk team enables us to get 1,000 more clients regularly to prebook their next appointment before they leave, and to book appointments more frequently.

Even though 1,000 may seem like a large number, it's less than 3 percent of our clientele (we have over 35,000 clients). If these 1,000 clients initiate a scheduling call, they come about every six to eight weeks and make about seven visits a year. With an average ticket of approximately $55, those 1,000 clients generate some $408,571 during the year.

If these 1,000 clients make their next appointment every four to six weeks by prebooking, we see a dramatic increase in the revenue they produce. These clients are still spending only $55 per visit, but they are now coming in 10 times a year and generating $572,000. That gain of $163,429 shows the power of prebooking.

As another advantage of focusing front desk duties, we realized a dramatic improvement in gift certificate sales, a big part of salon and spa revenues. In the weeks before Mother's Day or the holiday season, a busy spa can generate thousands of dollars in gift certificate sales.

Provided they have adequate time, well-trained guest care personnel can on their own increase the size of the average gift certificate sale.

Consider this scenario: A man walks in and asks how he can purchase a gift certificate for his wife. What the guest care person says next will determine the dollar amount of the gift certificate. If she says, "How much would you like that for?" he may say $75, and in minutes he will be on his way. Efficient, right? Wrong.

If instead the guest care person initially responds, "Let me show you our packages that have great value," and then goes on to explain her own favorite services and how much his wife would enjoy a facial, the husband may reconsider the amount he initially had in mind and increase it. Even if the gift certificate is for the same amount he would originally have spent, the spa benefits if the guest care personnel can get him to specify a facial or massage for that same value. If he gives his wife a $75 gift certificate, she will apply it to the service she routinely gets and she won't receive anything new or additional; all her husband did was prepay for the service. But if he gives her a gift certificate for a spa service, she may experience something new; now she received a gift, and the salon increased its revenue. Another added benefit is that the husband feels better about his gift. If his wife returns thrilled, he's more likely to buy another certificate in the future and less likely to complain about how she's spending her money because he will know how special it is.

Another excellent example of having a dedicated person to upsell the customer's average ticket is the sommelier, better known as the wine steward in the restaurant industry. Because of their extensive training and knowledge, they are able confidently to upsell the customer to the best available bottle of wine to complement his or her dinner choice. They can educate the consumer on why a particular bottle is valued higher. They can also recommend aperitifs, dessert wines, and ports. Someone who is excited about a particular product he or she has tasted or experienced makes the consumer excited about it too and more apt to try it. Once patrons have a good experience with the sommelier's choices, they are likely to depend on them for future choices as well.

## Obtain Client Information

In 1999 we discovered that out of 8,000 new clients, 535 of them did not give us their addresses because we failed to ask them to fill out an information card. That doesn't look too bad on the surface, because we got 93 percent of our new clients to fill out the card, but, out of the 535 clients who didn't fill out an information card, only 197, or 37 percent, ever returned. Our retention rate among clients who do fill out a card is 70 percent—one of the highest in the industry.

One of the most important things to do in your Secret Service system is to make sure you gather your clients' personal information. Without it, you cannot send a thank you card after the first visit. You cannot call to see if the first visit was everything the client anticipated. You cannot send a birthday card with an invitation to come in and pick up a birthday present. You cannot send newsletters to inform the client of everything going on at your business. You cannot send out follow-up mailings and incentives to lure back those clients who have not returned after several months.

Having a dedicated greeter and hostess position enables a business to obtain vital client information in an efficient manner, which in turn increases your new-client retention. Dedicate someone to making sure the customer's arrival is handled cheerfully and promptly. This is especially important at a place such as a doctor's or dentist's office, where the visit doesn't carry the same kind of excitement that other places can create. This could help reduce stress and related anxiety about the client's experiences.

At check-out, all new clients receive a new-client package, which includes a menu of services, the latest newsletter, a magnet, and a "How Did We Do?" card that asks them how their first experience went, what they liked best, and what they would like to change. How do we know who is a new client? Our computer system gives us pop-up notes identifying new clients, and their names are entered into our appointment book in a different color.

## Use The Customer's Name

A Secret Service system with a major impact is the way we incorporate the client's name into the processes of scheduling an appointment, checking in, and checking out. This is a policy from Marriott Desert Springs in Palm Springs, California. At every customer interaction, the Marriott staff member uses the customer's name at least four times.

We instituted this system after the size of our salon and spa expanded from 2,000 to 8,000 square feet. Our clients' biggest complaint suddenly was that nobody knew them any more. We heard this complaint from clients coming in twice a week, as well as from those coming every 4 to 6 weeks. Both groups feel they are our very good clients.

What if a new hostess asks Mrs. Smith, who visits us twice a week, "Have you ever been to John Robert's before?" Mrs. Smith, who knows almost everyone's first and last names, would look at the new hostess and say, "Honey, have I ever been here before? Have *you* ever been here before?"

When we expanded, we increased our guest care team from five to twenty almost overnight. We needed to make sure we didn't offend any of our customers, especially our best ones. We needed low turnover, which would result in our guest care team eventually learning many of our clients' names. We also needed to train this team well.

At John Robert's, every guest care person now makes an attempt to say the client's name at least four times when the client is checking in, checking out, or scheduling an appointment. This simple procedure has helped us eliminate virtually all complaints about not feeling recognized.

For example, when Mrs. Smith walks in, the hostess says, "Welcome, Mrs. Smith. I just notified Stacy that you have arrived. Mrs. Smith, can I hang up your jacket and get you a cup of hot coffee? What do you take in your coffee, Mrs. Smith? Would you like to change into a smock before Stacy comes to get you, Mrs. Smith?"

## Utilize Downtime

Downtime can be a concern when you separate the front desk functions. Now that each staff member is focused on only one task, the likelihood of downtime is much greater. You need to create a system to utilize that time. Good service companies use downtime to spend more time on the phone with callers. For example, a confirmation call is a great opportunity to inform the customer of additional appointments that are available when they are coming in, or tell them of special promotions they can take advantage of. With the dramatic decline in the stock market in the past two years, many financial service companies have adopted an aggressive customer service approach as they understand how critical it is to develop and maintain a stronger bond with their clients than ever before. Not only did they not have time before, but it also wasn't as necessary.

At John Robert's, call-center personnel utilize downtime to perform call-backs to new clients, make confirmation calls, write thank you cards, and send gift certificates to clients who refer new clients to us. Check-out personnel and hostesses utilize downtime to create new-client packages, straighten the products on display, and clean glass doors and counters.

The most important thing we want these departments to do during downtime is to provide added services to the clients who are in the salon so that we can implement every phase of the Customer Experience Cycle 100 percent of the time. It's a great system on paper, but it's worthless if it's acted on only some of the time. By creating separate centers, we now ensure that the guest care team has the time to perform all of these tasks.

## Create Efficiencies

Consider what I call voice-maze: You call a big company and are told to hit 1 for this, 2 for that. After you hit 1, they give you another menu, and that leads to another menu. It seems it will never stop. The system tells you to enter your account number (usually 15 digits), your zip code, and the last four digits of your Social Security number; you wait, and a human finally picks up the phone only to ask you for your account number. From the customer's perspective, this seems inefficient.

In contrast, consider McDonald's incredible efficiencies. At other fast-food drive-throughs, it takes on average three minutes from the moment you place your order until the moment you receive it. The average time at McDonald's is 90 seconds. That difference may be small, but at lunchtime, when there are 10 cars in line and you're hungry, you notice the difference. McDonald's even anticipates that you won't have the exact change and has the change ready.

Speedier drive-through times equal growth for Wendy's fast food restaurants. Wendy's instituted a new "Service Excellence" operations program in 2000 that dramatically improved their drive-through efficiencies. The nation's number 3 hamburger chain looked literally to drive sales growth through their drive-through sales. Their pick-up window generates 55% of their total sales, and another 15% is takeout, so nearly three quarters of their revenue is from carry out. Wendy's figured out if they could get more cars through the drive-through during peak times, then obviously sales would increase considerably.

The Service Excellence program creates labor efficiencies through such strategies as cross-training employees, providing adequate staffing levels in the restaurants, and using timing mechanisms and improved monitors at the drive-throughs. Many franchises have seen a substantial reduction in the length of time it takes for each car to go through, varying from 10 seconds to more than one minute. Because their growth is so sensitive to the productivity of their pick-up window, they are putting much more emphasis on tracking data for analyzing the causes of slowdowns and bottlenecks at the drive-throughs.

## Practice Your Secret Service System

Practice makes permanent.

*—Dale Carnegie*

I learned the importance of practice and efficiency when I was a driver for United Parcel Service. I spent the first two days of driver training in a classroom, learning how the truck was loaded. I spent the third day in an empty warehouse, where my supervisor had me sit in a truck and start the vehicle. The procedure was very specific: I fastened my seatbelt, put the truck in neutral, and released the emergency brake. Next I learned to put the truck in first gear with my right hand while putting on the emergency brake with my left hand. Another simultaneous maneuver followed: I turned the ignition off with my right hand while I took off my seatbelt with my left hand.

After I did this for about 15 minutes, it got really boring.

"What's next?" I asked my supervisor.

"That's it."

"I'm done for the day?"

"No, that's all you're supposed to do for the next two hours."

Those were the longest two hours of my life, but after a week on the road, I realized that was the most beneficial training I could have received. I used that drill hundreds of times every day, with every delivery and pickup, and I got really good at simultaneously putting the truck in gear, putting on the emergency brake, turning off the ignition, and unbuckling my seatbelt. It's amazing how much time was saved by mastering such simple movements.

**Incorporating Secret Service into your front line**

- Raise the awareness of your entire team to the critical role your front line plays in providing unforgettable customer service.
- Try to isolate major roles and make people specialists so they can go the extra mile, which should result in higher sales and bookings.
- Make it easy for staff to offer add-on sales, as well as for customers to take advantage of such.
- Provide dialogue that makes the customer feel special and convey that you are able to take as much time as possible to accommodate them.
- Arm your staff with scripts and answers to the most frequently asked questions and then repeatedly test them on it to ensure they answer these sensitive questions correctly.
- Create a system that ensures every customer has the opportunity to schedule future appointments/reservations with you prior to his or her departure.
- Make sure the front line gets all customer information, updates it, and incorporates names and personal information when dealing with customers.
- Have systems set up for people to utilize their downtime.

# CHAPTER 4

# What Are We Really Selling?

## Making It an Experience

The experience is remembered long after the price is forgotten.

How do you compete? Do you offer the lowest price, fastest service, convenience, a captive audience, or superior service? The answer will determine what your competitive advantage ultimately is. What you and your staff perceive that you sell will at the end of the day be what your customer buys.

### The Royal Palm

There are hotels and motels that rent their rooms for $39.99. They are selling a product—a room with a bed, TV, bathroom, and shower, no more, no less. Then you have the Royal Palms Hotel & Casitas in Phoenix, Arizona, an award-winning resort and hotel with rooms starting at $329 a night. They do not sell rooms. Because if it was a room you were looking for, they too have the bed, TV, bathroom, and shower, but for nearly $300 more. I am sure their mattresses are comfortable, but perhaps not $300 more comfortable.

The Royal Palm is one of the most sought after resorts anywhere. First, and most obviously, the accommodations are beautiful, featuring Spanish Colonial architecture, with every imaginable amenity. But it is the attention to detail on the part of their staff that makes their $300 plus a night rooms seem to be a great value and the reason why so many people return. For example, after booking a reservation for a corporate outing, someone from the hotel will contact someone from that corporation and arrange to have her send the hotel a picture of that person's family, prior to his arrival. The picture is displayed somewhere in the client's room.

The Royal Palms has a full-time Director of Romance to facilitate the ultimate romantic experience. According to the Travel Industry of America, 20 percent of all U.S. adults traveled for a romance-related reason during 2001—honeymoons, weddings, anniversary celebrations, and romantic getaways. Besides being a resort known for corporate meetings and business conventions, the Royal Palms Hotel wanted to tap into a growing market as a popular romantic destination. Their Director of Romance has put them on the romance map by not only ordering flowers and dinner reservations, but also offering advice on love matters, especially for the romantically challenged.

What has this reputation done for their business? They have orchestrated over 200 marriage proposals, thousands of anniversary celebrations, and countless birthday memories. They have enhanced these special memories with violinists, flamenco guitarists, poem readers, diamond-lace desserts, white doves, in-room massage, breakfast in bed, bubble baths surrounded by candlelight and topped with rose petals, astrology readings for couples, a rose petal turndown, champagne and chocolate covered strawberries, and airplanes spelling proposals in the sky. They sell the total experience.

## Ozaukee Bank

When you think of banks, you don't exactly think of an experience. What comes to mind are sterile lobbies, desks, and long lines. The Ozaukee Bank in Grafton, Wisconsin looks like a luxurious family room, with a fireplace, multiple TV screens, gourmet coffee, home decorating magazines and books to browse or buy, a video play area for children, computer terminals for customers, and oak floors and woodwork. The bank also has an online vacation planning station, as well as redecorating experts who conduct seminars on installing a faucet or stenciling. All this demonstrates that the bank offers more than check-cashing service and savings accounts.

In addition to these amenities, customers who want to try banking online but are wary of the technology can sit down, sip a cup of coffee, and have a bank employee take them through a hands-on lesson about doing their business with Ozaukee Bank over the Internet. This bank knows that it must create cozier, friendly environments, as financial institutions seek more customers in an increasingly competitive industry. As technology has created conveniences via internet banking and automated teller machines, it also has reduced personal contact between many bankers and their customers. Now more than ever, it is vital for banks to make people aware of their products and services. The Ozaukee Bank branch even made the drive-through an experience. While customers wait to cash their checks or make deposits or withdrawals, they can watch news and other programs on the TV monitors that have been mounted along auto lanes. This bank knows that it is selling not only bank experiences, but experiences as a whole.

## John Robert's

We ask new employees, "What do we sell?" They answer, "Haircuts, manicures, facials, and massages." I tell them, "If we sold only haircuts, manicures, facials, and massages, we would have been out of business years ago."

While I believe our services are second to none, in nearly every case our prices are anywhere from 50 percent to 300 percent higher than those of our competitors. Our $100 haircuts are excellent, but are they three times better than those given by a salon in the same shopping center that charges $25 for a haircut? We don't deceive ourselves by thinking we are the only ones who do great work, because many good salons have very talented hairdressers.

So how can our hairdresser who charges $100 for a haircut be totally booked for the next two months while a hairdresser at a salon nearby charges $25 and has six openings today? The reason is that we sell an experience. Clients can go to many places to get a good haircut or manicure for less. However, as a result of our Customer Experience

Cycle, our clients feel that our service, or their experience, has more value.

The phrase "Time is money" is not quite accurate. If time were money, all salons would earn the same amount for their haircuts. But that isn't the case, because value is money. We make people feel that our $100 experience has great value.

## Determine Your Point of Difference

Alaska Airlines has gone after a certain niche market that many airlines have totally ignored, thus giving them a point of difference. The airline has made significant efforts to attract the unaccompanied juvenile passenger. Children represent a growing market for airlines. In 2001, the Air Transport Association estimated that some seven million passengers were children. Some children fly so frequently that they are VIPs in the frequent fliers clubs. Handling unaccompanied children generates extra revenue on top of the ticketed air fare. Most major airlines charge an extra fee of between $30 and $75 each way for an unaccompanied child.

The airline offers a private, unmarked lounge, similar to a family room furnished with couches and overstuffed chairs, a high definition television, and a stack of coloring books. Their goal is to make sure the children on connecting flights are safe, secure, and happy and that their parents book them on that airline again.

Alaska Airlines has also developed a system that can pinpoint the location of children at any time during their trip. The system is similar to the one used for tracking packages. The child tracking system requires every employee who escorts a child to sign in when he or she picks the child up and sign out when he or she releases the child to another Alaska employee. The child's progress is tracked manually and through the airline's reservations computer system.

## Concentrate on the Customer Experience

The client is paying for her experience, not yours. You must leave yours at home.

It's critical that everyone on your team realizes that you are in the experience business. In other words, as employees they must leave their personal baggage at the door and deliver exceptional service every day to every client. Although we have many upscale clients, our average client is middle-class and works extremely hard. To many people, we may be their "trip to Paris" this year; they cannot afford to go to Europe, but they can and do ask their family or friends to buy them a day of pampering at John Robert's. When someone buys them a day of pampering, they are ecstatic. They schedule it 6 months in advance, book their sisters as well, arrange for sitters, and make a day of it. What if the manicurist had an argument with her boyfriend the night before and is not having a good day? What if she is running 20 minutes late and sharing every detail of her breakup with clients? We just ruined this woman's trip to Paris.

Joseph Pine and James Gilmore said it best in *The Experience Economy:* Work is theatre and every business a stage. If you look at your business and every other business this way, it gives you a whole new perspective. Pine and Gilmore tell you to pretend that your business charges admission just to get in. When you do this exercise, it's amazing how creative you become in making sure you provide an experience that justifies the price of admission. Then you implement all these new experiences throughout your business. Think of the fabulous deal your clients will get if you decide not to charge admission.

## Volkswagon

Volkswagen AG's Autostadt spent $417 million to build a new facility in Wolfsburg, Germany, that consists of a museum, six restaurants, a hotel, and several pavilions showing off all the VW group's brands—all in efforts to transform industry stereotype from just another dealership that sells cars to an auto buying experience extravaganza. Autostadt teamed up with the Ritz-Carlton as their 174-room on-site hotel, trying to transfer the standard of service offered by the hotel industry to the car industry. It's no wonder that the Autostadt now serves as a tourist attraction, selling souvenirs and car accessories. They even charge an entry fee, $11.78 per person, and attract more than one million visitors a year.

## U.S. Cellular

U.S. Cellular in Chicago trains their call centers to imagine the smiles on customers' faces. And if a customer wants a high-level answer to a problem, they can direct that customer through to the CEO. This unusual policy has resulted in a customer even contacting the CEO at his home to resolve a problem. The practice is a key reason why the 20-year-old company, which boasts 3.4 million customers, has only a 1.8 percent attrition rate, which is among the lowest in the industry.

U.S. Cellular recently installed a rate plan analyzer to help customers figure out if they're on the right plan or not. Their call centers routinely call subscribers, especially those on older plans, to make sure they're happy with their service.

U.S. Cellular concentrates more on effectiveness than efficiency. Their customer service department's goal is to provide customer delight, rather than complete a call in under seven minutes.

## Cooperstown

> Never save your best pitcher for tomorrow, for tomorrow it may rain.
>
> —Leo Durocher

The Pine & Gilmore exercise totally changes the way you look at how businesses conduct themselves. For example, I took my son Johnni to the Baseball Hall of Fame in Cooperstown, New York. We are huge baseball fans, so this was an exciting trip for us.

Every store in Cooperstown sells baseball merchandise of some sort: baseball cards, personalized bats, jerseys, pictures, and various other baseball memorabilia. The Hall of Fame and Double Day Baseball Field are also located in Cooperstown.

The Otesaga Hotel, a beautiful accommodation, is missing huge opportunities to create an experience that baseball fans would never forget. As the bellhop escorted us to our rooms, we started asking him all types of questions. Had he ever met any Hall of Famers? What stories did he have to tell? His answers were thrilling. Once asked, he told us how every person ever inducted into the Hall of Fame has stayed at the Otesaga Hotel. He told us which bar Babe Ruth frequented and where other legends had played poker.

After he left, I started to wonder who had stayed in our room and slept in this bed. Why doesn't the Otesaga Hotel have a list of all the players who stayed in this room, maybe with their signatures, on a room registry, framed and mounted to the wall of this room? What if they named rooms after Hall of Famers? For example, room 714 could be the Babe Ruth room because he hit 714 home runs, a record that held for decades until Hank Aaron broke it. The Otesaga Hotel could also train every bellman to have a scripted speech while he escorts people to their rooms, telling them facts and stories about the hotel and the Hall of Famers. Every baseball fan would love that.

The Hall of Fame was great, but the experience in its theater could be improved. Fans can visit the theater for free; every hour a film is shown on the history of baseball. You need to arrive 15 minutes beforehand and wait in a theater designed like the grandstands at a baseball park. Why not have vendors sell hot dogs, peanuts, cotton candy, and soda while you wait? Or have a comedian dressed like an usher, to entertain people and get the crowd to sing "Take Me Out to the Ball Game." The same film is shown every hour, all day long. Why not change the film every hour? With these experiences, the Hall of Fame could definitely charge extra for the theater, and people would go back several times a day to be entertained with different shows.

## Nordstrom's
Service is given; hospitality is felt.

—Jim Sullivan

Like so many other people, I go to Nordstrom's because of the quality of their clothes as well as their outstanding customer service. I don't have much time to shop for clothes, so I make two trips a year. Nordstrom's is usually more expensive but worth it because of the no-hassle experience. They take anything back, no questions asked, no receipt needed. Alterations are free. I can take as many items as I want into the dressing room, and the salesperson checks constantly to see if I need different sizes. As a result, I may purchase 12 out of 20 items I try. It's a successful shopping day for me, quick and effective.

Afterward I visited the national department store I used to frequent before Nordstrom's opened in our area. So much merchandise was crammed in that I could hardly walk between the racks, let alone sort through items. The salesclerk made it a point to say I could take only a few items at a time into the fitting room. When I needed him I couldn't find him, so I put the clothes down and left.

If Nordstrom's had limited the items in the fitting room, I would never have had the patience to go out, get more items, and buy more. A store that limits items not only limits sales but also insults and inconveniences the 99 percent of its customers who don't steal. Nordstrom's creates a consistently memorable experience, and that's where I continue to shop.

## Doctor's and Dentist's Offices

Doctors' offices are notorious for poor customer service. One pediatrician we called had office hours Monday through Friday, 9:00 A.M. to 3:00 P.M., and was closed late afternoons, evenings, and Saturdays. Their patients are children who are in school from 9 to 3. When will doctors catch up with the rest of the world and have hours that accommodate today's society? Doctors force their patients to take days off from work and to have their children miss school for appointments.

Inconvenient office hours are not the only customer service issue the medical industry has. I know dozens of people who stopped going to a doctor they loved because the staff at the front desk was so poorly trained. The doctor could have the best knowledge, care, and bedside manner, yet be too busy to realize what is going on at the front desk. More than a few times, when I try to book an appointment, the receptionist gives me a look that says, "You want an appointment when?"

On entering the doctor's office, getting noticed is almost impossible. The receptionist is typically on the phone or the computer, and under no circumstances will she look up even to acknowledge my presence or indicate that she will be with me momentarily.

Every doctor's and dentist's office could definitely benefit from having separate and specialized areas for check-in, check-out, and phone calls, especially offices that are extremely large and congested. If I am leaving and need to schedule a future appointment but see lots of people at the counter, I decide to call from my car so I don't have to be delayed even longer. I end up on hold for 10 minutes because the same office staff who answer the phones are checking patients in and out.

More than anyone else in business, doctors' offices need to train their staff in better customer service because of the stress and anxiety associated with going to the doctor. Who wants to be there or looks forward to it? Wouldn't it ease your anxiety if a hostess greeted you with a warm smile and a hello? What if the waiting room were more entertaining and interactive, instead of feeling so gloomy? The television could show a comedy to help lift your spirits. Computer stations could offer trivia games or Internet access so you could check your e-mail and surf the Web. Phones and fax machines could enable you to utilize wait times productively. If the waiting room were laid out like a Starbucks, you could get a cappuccino or espresso and choose from a great selection of books to read while you wait. You know you have to wait, but you wouldn't mind it as much. If that were your doctor's office, would you still dread going? If waiting is inevitable, then businesses need to reduce the cost of the customer's wait time or enable the customer to use that time as productively as possible.

Dr. Scott Rose, a dentist in Solon, Ohio, has built his office around comfort. He designed the office so every aspect—from sight and sound to smell and touch—would be geared toward comfort. His office has calming fountains, a wine-and-juice bar, massage chairs, aromatherapy in the treatment rooms, personal headphones, blankets, warm face towels, fresh flowers every week, candles, and unique upscale magazines that are never more than a month old. He tries to be the Ritz Carlton of dentistry.

Other dentists have pinball machines in their waiting room and televisions hanging from the ceiling in treatment rooms so patients can watch television while their teeth are cleaned or worked on.

## Car Dealerships

Think about cars and customer loyalty. Stacy and I keep our cars for 2 to 3 years, and when our lease is up we usually get something different.

We shop for a new car quite often, yet we have never leased from the same dealership twice. We haven't even leased the same make of car twice in a row. Why? Because no car dealership or salesman or manufacturer has ever bothered to make us loyal. Apart from the survey 30 days after we sign the lease, asking us to rate the dealership, we never hear from any of them again until a month before our lease expires. Then we get a letter telling us the formalities for turning in a lease or purchasing our car.

Of all businesses, I think it should be easiest for car dealerships to create customer loyalty. But I have never received a personalized thank you letter from a salesman or a dealership. The salesman always makes it a point, as soon as I have leased a car, to tell me I will get a survey and to ask me to give him high marks. Do you think if he sent me a thank you note it might prompt me to give him high marks? A car customer for life is worth thousands of dollars, much more if you consider relatives and referrals.

I have approached many car dealerships to investigate some type of networking, so that every time they sell or lease a new car, they send their customer a gift certificate to John Robert's. It amazes me that the majority of dealerships don't see the value in sending the customer a thank you gift. That's the problem: They apparently think of the person who just drove off the showroom floor not as a new customer but as a past customer who will have no value for at least 2 or 3 years.

Besides sending a thank you note or gift, car dealerships have many opportunities to put the dealership's name continuously in front of the client with reminders about oil changes and other scheduled service needs, and with newsletters that give useful tips on car care, spotlight salesmen, tell what the dealership is doing in the community, inform you about new models to get you excited about your next car, and possibly even offer incentives for upgrading your current lease. Would this kind of communication and service increase the chances of creating repeat customers tenfold? Some car dealerships do this, but they are typically only the higher end dealers. Why isn't something so inexpensive and so effective done by all dealers? Instead dealers spend a huge amount of money on advertising that chases new business when they could retain so many more of their previous customers for the cost of postage.

## Tim Lally Chevrolet

Tim Lally Chevrolet of Bedford Heights, Ohio, has made car buying an enjoyable event. Customers and their families can take advantage of a large play area for children, like those at McDonald's, as well as a movie theater, beauty salon, beverage-and-refreshment center (with self-serve cappuccino and popcorn machines), and an enormous showroom. The waiting area has comfortable furniture, windows to view the service area, four computer stations with Internet access, a gym complete with a locker room and showers, and an Alamo rent-a-car office. The staff has two kitchens and dining areas: one off the showroom floor, and one off the service area, for mechanics.

## Saturn

If you want a true car-buying experience, go to Saturn. First, there's no pressure on customers, partly because commission is based not on individual performance but on the entire team. Another reason is that Saturn wants to impress its customers so they return for another Saturn in three or four years. When someone buys a car, Saturn makes it an event. A picture is taken of the customer standing next to his new car and holding a congratulatory sign (the picture is mailed with a thank you card). The customer receives a surprise gift, and each salesperson does something different, maybe balloons attached to a coffee mug filled with candy, or a bottle of champagne. Saturn has a specially lit spot in the showroom called the Jewel Box. The customer's newly purchased car, whether new or used, is taken through this spot. The car really shines, the customer gets a special feeling as the car comes off the showroom floor, and everyone applauds as the customer drives away.

## Florists

Make the kids happy and you'll get the parents. That's the philosophy of Green Mansions Florist in Centreville, Virginia. Barbara Fitz has created a children's area that has a fish tank, a miniature picnic table, toys, and books. When busy parents stop in after work to buy flowers, they can take their time and not worry about their children. With experiences like this, families remember the florist shop and keep coming back.

## Pike Place Market

> Greatness is ordinary people producing extraordinary results.
>
> —Jimmy Valvano

You may have heard about Pike Place Market in Seattle, Washington. It has been made famous by a best-selling book, *Fish: A Remarkable Way to Boost Morale and Improve Results.* The employees of Pike Place Market have turned a mundane work environment into an enjoyably productive atmosphere. They discovered that a playful, attentive, and engaging attitude leads to more energy, enthusiasm, productivity, and creativity. Several other fish markets are nearby, but none draws the attention and crowds every day the way Pike Place Market does.

When a customer places an order, the employee who takes it yells out the order and destination, "One salmon flying away to Minnesota," as he throws the large fish 20 feet to another employee, who packages the fish and rings up the sale. Then all the other workers repeat in unison, "One salmon flying away to Minnesota." The workers behind the counter make a one-handed catch and bow to the applauding audience of people who have gathered and watch in amazement. This is just a sample of the entertainment that goes on at a company that sells fish.

## Everybody's Grocery Store

> We are here to say yes to people, and we just happen to sell groceries as well.
>
> —John Dey

John Dey is the owner of Everybody's Grocery Store in Fairfield, Iowa. Despite its remote location and competition from two major chains, Everybody's Grocery Store does more than $5 million in sales annually. How do they do it? They succeed the old-fashioned way, with old-fashioned customer service that the rest of us can learn from. Everybody's Grocery Store has focus groups with customers. If just one customer wants a certain product, Everybody's orders a case of it so that it's available for that one customer. The entire staff meets every month to talk about customer service.

The best companies act as a resource center for their clientele, both in offering additional services and products themselves and in referring their customers to companies that can provide related services and products that they do not but that still benefit their customers. This type of service demonstrates that you are looking out for your customer's best interests, which solidifies your relationship with that customer like nothing else can.

Here's a great example of how a company can be a resource. One day I got my monthly bill from D & D Cleaners, which cleans our Solon salon, and saw a note attached. I expected it to say either that I was late with a payment or that D & D was raising its rates. To my surprise, the note told me that the staff noticed my carpet needs a good cleaning, that it's time for my floor to be stripped and waxed, and that it's time for me to change my furnace filters.

I thought "impressive . . . they are stimulating additional sales," but to my surprise, the last line of the note said, "While we do not perform these services, if you need someone to, we would be happy to recommend some companies that do." Now I was really impressed. These people are looking out for me, even when it can't benefit them. The first thing I did was to call D & D and ask them to clean my Mayfield salon, too.

## Travel Agencies

Today travel agencies are considered an endangered species. With so many customers taking their business to the Internet, you would think that travel agencies would go to great lengths to demonstrate how they differ and how they can provide valuable services unavailable on the Internet, but I don't see that happening. I don't think as many people would have chosen to handle their own travel arrangements on the Internet if they had been getting service that's difficult to duplicate.

For instance, after I have booked a flight with a travel agent, he has never asked me what else I needed. I always have to be the one who initiates a request for a hotel room or a rental car. A good travel agent who offered to take care of anything I needed—be it a hotel, transportation, sightseeing, or tickets for events—would not be feeling vulnerable right now.

As another example, many of us booked our honeymoon with a travel agent. How many agencies contact us a few months before an anniversary to offer to help plan an anniversary getaway? Or, when an agency has booked a trip, how many agencies call a few days ahead or send an e-mail to let us know they confirmed our departing and arriving times, as well as our hotel and car rental, to ensure that everything is still on schedule? This e-mail could also tell us the weather forecast so we know how to pack. They could provide a traveler's checklist that reminds us not to forget a passport, driver's license, or traveler's checks. Agencies could also provide tips on packing and could suggest must-see places and the city's best restaurants.

Travel agencies could ask you about your favorite destinations (e.g., Las Vegas) and your dream destinations (e.g., Hawaii), and send you information when they have special rates to those locations. In other words, a travel agency could be considered a travel concierge. If travel agencies did all that, would any of us spend time doing it ourselves? If you know of an agency that does this, please let me know.

Travel agents may say their margins are too small to be able to do this. After the initial setup, however, nearly all of this takes virtually no additional time. Once a document has been created listing the sights and best restaurants for every major city, then all that's needed is to cut and paste the appropriate items into an e-mail and hit the send button. Each e-mail can have a link to a local weather report. If the airlines felt that travel agencies benefited the airlines' business by increasing the amount of travel people do, the airlines wouldn't be trying to squeeze the agencies out. And with this kind of service, a travel agency could easily justify service charges to increase its profit margins.

One travel agency providing concierge type service is Professional Travel, a chain with offices across the United States. They provide weekend upgrade service to their VIP customers at no charge. They sweep their reservation system every Friday to identify every traveler who is scheduled to depart on Monday and then determine their level of frequent flier status. Since most frequent flier programs enable their elite level members to call and reserve first class upgrades within 24 to 48 hours of flight departure, they provide this for them, so they don't have to remember to do it themselves. They have a representative who works on the weekend and they pay her a per call fee to call the airlines directly and get their VIP clients upgraded for their Monday departures. Professional Travel also keeps a database on their customers that captures information such as preferred seating, frequent flier numbers, and particular needs of children and spouses.

## Fredric's Corporation

A popular and insidious myth says that different rules apply to those businesses that don't deal directly with the consumer, such as distributors and manufacturers. Owners of these businesses feel limited in how they can take care of their clients.

Fredric Holzberger, CEO and founder of Fredric's Corporation, doesn't feel that way. Fredric's is a distributor of Aveda products, and its customers are salons across the Midwest and elsewhere. This company has inspired me as it continuously raises the bar on exceeding customer expectations day in and day out.

First, Fredric's account executives work in our salons on a weekly basis to help them increase our retail sales, and they are available at any time to train our new employees on product knowledge. I appreciate any opportunity my staff has to experience the Fredric's team, from simply observing how they answer the phones to watching them work at a show or seminar. Their attention to detail is total, and nothing you ask of them is a problem.

It's easy to see why all employees of Fredric's Corporation are so oriented to customer service. Fred is a master at customer service. One time Fred visited a salon two days before a grand opening to see how things were going. He found total mayhem. The salon didn't look as if it would be ready to open in 2 weeks, let alone 2 days. The look on the salon owner's face was one of pure fear. Fred immediately got on his phone, had his next 2 days of appointments rescheduled, and had several of his staff do likewise. Fred and his team worked the next 2 days and nights helping this salon open on time. At the grand opening nobody could tell there had ever been a problem.

When we had our own grand opening for our new salon and spa, Fred couldn't have been more accommodating. He sent 10 employees from Cincinnati to Cleveland for the entire week before our grand opening to help with anything we might need. They brought moving trucks to help us move equipment, furniture, and products from our old location to our new one. They also helped us set up for our grand opening and provided complimentary services.

The morning of our grand opening, I was proud of how well prepared we were until I realized our cleaning crew hadn't shown up that morning and the floors showed all the traffic. When Fred stopped in several hours before the opening to see how we were doing, he found me frantically trying to locate my cleaners to see if they were coming. Within 15 minutes Fred had his whole team cleaning the place, and he himself mopped the entire floor, all 8,000 square feet of it. That is Fred: no job is beneath him, and he will do whatever is required to take care of his customers. He is totally focused on customer service, and he demonstrates that nothing is too difficult, too lowly, or too much to do if it means satisfying a client. When a CEO personally sets that example, then the rest of the staff can only follow in his footsteps, which is the case at Fredric's Corporation.

Even though the Fredric's Corporation is one of the leaders in the beauty distribution industry primarily because of the intensive customer service training every employee must go through prior to ever interacting with any of their customers, it is the standard and legacy that their CEO sets that their entire organization feels an obligation to continue and enhance.

At Frederic's, every new employee must attend a week-long training seminar that covers how they provide legendary customer service. They don't stop there, however. Once a week, for one hour on Thursday afternoons, they close their business down, shut the phones off, and meet individually as departments and then as a group. They have an Annual Rejuvenation Meeting that reinforces the high level customer service culture, featuring renowned guest speakers. Another key policy at Fredric's that ensures the highest quality in customer service is the requirement that every employee must be cross-trained throughout the various departments, such as customer relations, order processing, accounting, graphic design, information technology, and so on. In addition Fredric's has focus groups with a different team of employees each month based on their anniversary and birthday dates. It's an excellent, yet simple system to get a wide variety of employees attending, enrolled, and heard.

Because I get such outstanding service from Fredric's Corporation, I deal exclusively with them for all the hair care products we use and sell. Why would I use anyone else if I get that kind of service? I give Fredric's over $500,000 in sales a year, but the critical point is this: Long before we were a great customer of theirs, Fredric's gave us unforgettable customer service.

## Guardian

My fire extinguisher company, Guardian, provides excellent service. To ensure that we meet city codes, Guardian knows the expiration dates on all my fire extinguishers and automatically services them and puts on the stamp needed for the fire marshal's inspections. I don't have to remember to call Guardian; they just handle it. Someone asked me if Guardian is expensive. I have no idea because I would never bother to do a price check. Guardian lifts a burden from me, and I have never been cited by the fire department. When the service is great, price becomes less important. Think about the places where you love to do business. Could you get the product or service cheaper somewhere else? Probably. Would you? It's not likely.

This type of service easily applies to other businesses, such as gutter cleaners and chimney sweeps. But many wait for the phone to ring instead of taking the initiative. This is another system that is so simple to implement into any service business. Keep a database or calendar of dates when customers are due for their next service. Most software systems today allow you to print these reports at the push of a button. On a weekly or monthly basis, run the report and follow up.

## Hospital Care

Set the standard for your competition. When you think of hospitals, do you think of customer service? If you have ever been to Griffin Hospital in Derby, Connecticut, customer service is the first thing that comes to mind. Griffin goes to extraordinary measures to please its patients and improve their spirits. For example, Griffin's entrance looks more like a hotel than a hospital. Professional musicians are on site. There are no restricted visiting hours; people can visit any time of day. After listening to patients' wish lists, Griffin invested in having a company make double hospital beds to accommodate family members who want to stay overnight.

More and more hospitals are following this trend. After a recent and substantial renovation at Hillcrest Hospital in Mayfield Heights, Ohio, the entrance appears modeled on a mall design. The atrium offers an optical center, drug stores, hair salon, and coffee shop. Hillcrest is building a library that not only offers medical material for staff but also serves as a resource for patients, providing a better understanding of the condition for patient or family, including books for children.

Catherine Leary, Hillcrest's Chief Operating Officer, understands the anxiety associated with coming to a hospital. "At Hillcrest, we want to be a healing and nurturing environment for the patients and their families as well as our employees." As a result, Hillcrest constantly provides its staff with seminars on providing excellent customer service to patients. Any complaint Hillcrest receives is followed up until the patient and the hospital feel everyone is satisfied; complaints are tracked in a book called the Gift Book, so named in reference to Catherine Leary's philosophy that every complaint is a gift and should be treated as such. She says, "A complaint is like a consultant giving us vital information for free."

## Credit Card Companies

Credit card companies do a great job of stimulating additional sales. Some credit card companies automatically increase your limit without your having to apply for it. They have also mastered the frequent buyer programs with perks such as cash back or airline miles incentives. One of the best services they provide is to call you when there is unusually high activity on your card. They could do more. What if they called when you hadn't used the card for some time, to make sure you were happy with them? What if they offered to put your company logo on your credit card, the way some credit card companies now offer to put your favorite sports team's logo on your card? A business owner would love to offer all his employees an opportunity to sign up for this card, and it would be viewed as an added benefit of employment. What great branding and advertising it would be every time they used it.

## Napa Valley Grille

An example of a frequent buyer program is the Napa Valley Grille. Napa Valley Grille, a national restaurant, has an award program called Café Club. Anyone can become a member and each time you dine at one of their locations, earn points that can use toward different prizes. For example, every time you reach 250 points you will receive $25 toward your next meal, or you can save those points for something bigger like a hot air balloon ride or night out on the town.

## Provide Win–Win Opportunities

Many businesses that go to the customer can use a win–win technique that boosts the company's profitability and gives the customer a discount. For example, a landscaper could use this technique very effectively in a new development when quoting a price for weekly lawn maintenance. His base price might be $160 a month per house, and for every five additional houses he gets on that street, everyone's price would drop $5. If he got half of the street, let's say 40 hours of work, everyone's price would drop to $110 per month. That's quite a savings for the homeowners, and it's profitable for the landscaper, who typically spends much of the day in unproductive time driving between assignments and loading and unloading the trailer.

Let's say a two-man crew does twelve houses per day and averages two houses per neighborhood, which generates $1,900 a month in revenue. If the landscaper gets a sizable portion of one neighborhood, he has eliminated virtually all unproductive time and has tripled the number of houses he can do per day. Even if he only doubles his capacity and does twenty-four houses a day, his monthly revenue for that 1 day (of the week) jumps to $2,640, an increase of $740 a month. He could increase his income even more if customers want other services, such as landscape design or sprinkler systems.

How impressed would you be if a landscaper called you halfway through the summer to see how satisfied you are with his work? What if your landscaper mailed you a notice in September thanking you for your business and informing you of his snow plowing services available in February? Finally, what if he gave you for every referral (or two or three), not a discount on your current bill, but a gift certificate toward his services on a future contract? It almost guarantees that you are going to sign up with him again.

### Deciding What You Sell

- Determine what is your point of difference: price, convenience, upscale, and so on.
- Determine what it is that you are really selling, what it is your customers are really buying.
- Think of every customer interaction: how can it be more of an experience, what can you provide that makes it an event, from the phone call all the  way through the follow-up a few days after the purchase.
- Provide such a memorable performance that customers would be willing to pay an entrance fee just to be guest or a spectator.
- Develop a training program that fosters a feeling of theatre that enables your staff to see themselves as performers providing a show at every stage.
- Think of unavoidable customer inconveniences and turn them into memorable events. For example, wait times can be staged in a Starbucks atmosphere with online access or hold times can be spent being entertained by creative message on holds systems.
- Find ways to celebrate customers publicly to give them a VIP feeling.

# CHAPTER 5

# Drilling for Oil in Your Own Backyard:

## Marketing to Go Deeper with Existing Customers

Marketing and advertising are expensive. It's been said that half of it works, but nobody knows which half. To see great returns, focus more on keeping your current customers than on attracting new ones.

At John Robert's, every month we get between 800 and 1,000 new clients at one location, which is more than double what many salons get in a year's time. As a result, I am asked to do marketing seminars all over the United States. Although John Robert's has many effective and creative marketing programs that help us attract new clients, the first thing I tell the audience is not to advertise. Instead, market to your existing clientele: One of the best marketing techniques you can have is a really happy client.

Companies put considerable effort and money into targeting likely prospects, with most of them spending 80 to 90 percent of their advertising budget on attracting new clients. I have always found it far more cost-effective and profitable to market to people who are already customers. We spend more than 95 percent of our advertising budget on retaining our existing clients. The history you have with existing customers gives you many advantages over the competition. You know things nobody else knows about your customers: their preferences and idiosyncrasies. You can use this information to target your existing clients to produce additional sales and create long-term loyalty. In addition, if you take really good care of your existing clients, they will generate more new clients than any advertising campaign ever could.

If our existing clients become dissatisfied, then our advertising is merely replacing the clients we lost with new ones, exposing more people to inferior service who will then tell their family and friends how bad we are. So our marketing focus is on our current clients. I want three things from our existing clients: more visits, more dollars spent per visit, and more referrals.

Any one of these three things has a dramatic impact. For example, we have more than 35,000 clients, and our average client spends $55 a visit. If we could get one third of our clients to come one more time a year at an average ticket of $55, we would generate more than $635,000 in additional revenue. With that kind of growth, who needs to advertise or even worry about finding new clients?

Table 5–1 illustrates how much you can increase revenue by increasing your average ticket generated with your current client base. This example assumes 3,000 clients per month and shows a range of ticket prices. Whatever the price of your average sale, you can see that an increase of just 10 percent can significantly affect your bottom line.

This concept applies to virtually every industry.

**Table 5–1. Increasing your revenue by increasing your average ticket with your current client base**

| Average ticket | No. of clients per month | Total revenue | $$ increase per month | $$ increase per year |
|---|---|---|---|---|
| $30.00 | 3000 | $ 90,000 | | |
| $33.00 | 3000 | $ 99,000 | $ 9,000 | $108,000 |
| $36.30 | 3000 | $108,900 | $18,900 | $226,800 |
| $39.93 | 3000 | $119,790 | $29,790 | $357,480 |
| $43.92 | 3000 | $131,769 | $41,769 | $501,228 |
| $48.32 | 3000 | $144,946 | $54,946 | $659,351 |
| $53.15 | 3000 | $159,440 | $69,440 | $833,286 |

## Encourage Word-of-Mouth Marketing

Very rarely do we advertise to the general public. As with every business, our best source of advertising is word-of-mouth. So we found a way to make our clients work for us. When we first opened, we rewarded our clients every time they referred someone new with a $5 gift certificate. People felt appreciative and had an added incentive to speak well of us.

In 1995 we took it to the next level. We started a client referral contest and gave the client with the most referrals that year a day of pampering at John Robert's. Our clients really got into it. That year the winner had 11 referrals, and many clients tied at 10, 9, and 8.

In 1996 we increased the prize to a stay at a condo in Naples, Florida, for a week. This really got people excited. The winner had 16 referrals, and a dozen people were close runners-up. The 1997 grand prize was a cruise for two on the *Royal Caribbean*. You can't imagine the response we got. Our clients were practically bringing in busloads of people. The winner had 92 referrals, the person in second place had 90, and dozens of clients had totals in the 80s, 70s, and 60s. The 1998 grand prize was a 1-year lease for a new Monte Carlo.

Not one of our grand prizes cost us a penny. They were all generously donated by travel agencies and car dealers in exchange for their company's exposure to more than 30,000 John Robert's clients.

In addition to the referral contest, nearly every piece of literature that goes out to our clientele reminds them to refer others. We say things like, "The highest compliment we can receive is a referral of a family member or friend."

Marriott Vacation Club in Orlando, Florida, understands the power of referrals. As an incentive for referring new time-share customers, Marriott gives its existing clients Marriott Reward points that can be used at any Marriott location in the world. It's no wonder that nearly 40 percent of all new customers are referrals by existing time-share customers.

At the end of each year we review our top 500 clients and compare this list to the prior year's. In the past, one of our greatest frustrations was seeing how many clients we had lost from the previous year's top

500. That number was as high as 47 clients. While that's less than 10 percent, these clients spent anywhere from $2,000 to $7,500 a year. If they were our best clients, why were we losing them?

We realized that we actually have more opportunity to disappoint our best customers. Let's say we drop the ball 10 percent of the time: a hairdresser runs late or goes home sick, we double-book an appointment, or the client gets stuck in traffic and is so late that we can't accommodate her. Though we strive for perfection, many things can go wrong. If you visit the salon every six weeks, you visit eight times a year. If our disappointment rate is 10 percent, that means you would be unhappy with our service once every other year. That's tolerable. If you're one of our top 500 clients, however, you come in once a week, 52 times a year. A 10 percent rate means we disappoint you five times a year. That isn't so acceptable, especially for our best clients.

## Appreciate Your Best Clients More

While our retention rate for all clients is important, our retention rate for our top 500 clients is critical. First, we obviously always need to work on improving our service so we disappoint less. But we will still make mistakes occasionally, so it's important to have systems in place to accommodate the client for any trouble we caused (for details, see Chapter 7).

But that still isn't enough, so we decided to show our top 500 clients how much we appreciate them. During the holidays, we now send them three gifts of appreciation. The first is a $50 gift certificate to a five-star restaurant. We do this as a trade with the top 10 restaurants in Cleveland, which gives the restaurants as well as John Robert's an opportunity to gain high-end clients who feel it's worth it to pay top dollar for the right experience. We send these gift certificates to our clients with a letter saying we are sure they will enjoy this great restaurant because we know how much they enjoy first-class service. The restaurants reciprocate by sending their best customers a gift certificate to John Robert's.

The second gift we send to our top 500 is a gift certificate to John Robert's for a service they have never received even though they already love us and spend a great deal of money and time with us. We get them to experience something new and turn them on to that service. For example, at the end of 1999, we saw that the client who was no. 242 on our list had never received hair services at John Robert's, so we gave her a $50 gift certificate toward any hair service. One year later she had climbed from 242 to 2, and her spending with us increased from $2,500 to well over $7,000 a year.

The third and final gift is the least expensive but gets the most attention. We send each of our top 500 clients a $25 gift certificate to give to a family or friend who has never been to John Robert's. A number of our top clients work and live in upscale areas, and we want to gain access to their circle of family and friends. During the holidays, like most of us, they have long lists of people on their gift list. Our gift certificate helps them with that list and gives us the opportunity to gain new clients.

How successful is this plan? Of our top 500 clients in 1999, we retained 478. Our loss rate dropped to less than 5 percent, half of what it had been the year before. We hope and think we also improved our service, but we definitely know we improved the way we show our appreciation, which may result in our top clients being more forgiving if we do drop the ball. As a bonus, our appreciation plan boosted sales and increased our number of new clients.

## Reevaluate Your Secret Service Continually

We are always trying to redefine how well we can take care of our customers, especially the 20 percent who make up 80 percent of our business. We have recently introduced a new reward system for clients who have spent over a certain amount with us during the previous year. Clients who spend $1,000 or more now receive certain privileges. First, they get a 5 percent discount on gift certificates and products. Second, they get a 10 percent discount on gift certificates purchased for people who have never been to John Robert's, which is a double bonus: their 10 percent discount plus the $5 gift certificate we give everyone who refers someone new to John Robert's. Third, they receive the direct phone numbers and e-mail addresses of the managers of all three salons in the event of any difficulty getting an appointment or any need to communicate with them. We tell these clients that while we cannot guarantee that we will be able to accommodate them every time for an appointment, we will certainly do our best. We were surprised to find out that the third perk was the one clients value most, even though they generally use it only when they have a big event and urgently need an appointment. We want to make sure we are able to take care of these clients because if we don't, we know someone else will.

Our client newsletter is probably our most effective tool for going deeper with existing clients. This newsletter goes out quarterly to our entire database of more than 35,000 clients. It announces what we have done within our community, describes advance education our team has had, spotlights team members, promotes our contests and referral incentives, and makes our clients aware of services on promotion, gift certificates, and packages.

We schedule these newsletters, along with most of our marketing, to go out the last week of December, May, and August, to help drive additional business during our slower periods: January and February, June and July, and September and October. For instance, our holiday newsletter has incentives valid during January and February. Our newsletters are so effective that during the 2 weeks after sending out a newsletter, we have to staff our call centers with additional people to handle the incoming calls.

The Internet is another tool that we use to increase the frequency of our clients' visits. We began with a good website, where clients can request an appointment, purchase gift certificates, view the latest happenings, and so on. We have built on this by developing a way to notify clients of last-minute cancellations. Just before we close for the night, we review the next day's appointments for last-minute cancellations, and we send an e-mail that these slots have become available. For example, someone may have called at 7:30 P.M. and canceled a pedicure for 10:00 A.M. the next morning. During the summer, when pedicure appointments are filled well in advance, we will have several e-mail responses waiting when we open our doors the next morning. An unfilled appointment is like an empty airplane seat; once the plane takes off, you cannot resell that seat.

We also played off eBay.com by creating our own version on our website, called JR Charity Auction (all proceeds go to Rainbow Babies & Children's Hospital). Once a week we block off a prime-time appointment with one of our top operators, who is typically booked out weeks in advance. Clients who do not want to wait four weeks or more to get an appointment can go to our website and bid on an appointment within the week with that operator. This achieves three things: first, it benefits a worthy cause; second, it draws attention and activity to our website, where people can learn about other promotions; and third, it helps us determine that operator's next price increase.

One of our most powerful tools for stimulating spontaneous sales—those empty airplane seats—is our appointment easel, set up next to the hostess podium at our entrance. It displays all of the day's available appointments. Clients are so used to our being solidly booked that they never think to ask if there's an appointment available at the last minute. A client checking in for a 6:00 P.M. haircut can look at the easel and see a 7:00 P.M. manicure opening and take it. This idea was suggested by Lisa Adams, one of our employees, and it has been our most effective way to sell appointments that open up at the last minute.

## Capitalize on a Client's Lifetime Value

It's not losing one unhappy client that hurts you so much; it's all the potential clients who hear about your unhappy client's experience.

A client's lifetime value is so much more than most people think. Let's say that a client goes to the same salon and spa for 25 years, and that a good client spends $1,500 a year at our salon on services, products, and gift certificates. Also assume this client refers an average of two new people every year who spend just $500 a year each. Two new referrals a year for 25 years may seem like a lot to gain from one individual, but we're also including referrals made by the clients this person refers.

Figuring in all those facts, along with an annual 5 percent increase in cost of living, this original client who spends $1,500 a year is ultimately worth about $400,000. She would have spent $71,591 herself, and the clients she referred, each spending only $500 a year, would have brought in $325,000.

So when we disappoint a client, do not make it right, and the client decides never to return, we are losing not only a $50 haircut but also the potential to earn $400,000. We are also mindful of the additional damage an unhappy client can do with negative word-of-mouth to other potential lifetime clients. Time, money, and energy are obviously much better spent in retaining existing clients than in attracting new ones. In my view, the best marketing we do is customer follow-up and putting our name in front of them half a dozen times a year reminding them who we are, what we provide, and how much we care. This is anything from a thank you card after their first visit, to a quarterly newsletter, a $5 gift certificate thanking them for the referral, to a happy birthday card.

## Don't Discount

Discounting lowers the perceived value of products and services. Instead, we camouflage our discounting through vehicles that makes people think they either won our services or received them as a gift. I would rather give away a service than discount it.

As a good example of how we disguise a discount, every time a BMW dealer sells a new car, the owner receives a gift certificate to John Robert's. Similarly, we give gift certificates to travel agencies, realtors, mortgage lenders, jewelers, restaurants, and builders as a gift of appreciation to their high-end customers.

We target all our marketing to stimulate business during our slower months. A prime target is virtually across the street from our Mayfield location: Hillcrest Meridia Hospital, which employs more than 2,000 doctors, nurses, and administrative staff. At the end of August we had their Chief Operating Officer send every employee a $25 gift certificate to John Robert's as a gesture of employee appreciation at no charge. That helped spark a typically slow September and October, and in addition we really benefited in November and December, when many of Hillcrest's employees booked repeat services and purchased gift certificates for family and friends.

Fishbowls are another effective marketing technique for gaining new clients. We put fishbowls in high-end restaurants, with a sign that says "Drop in your business card to win a day of pampering." Each month we collect hundreds of business cards of professionals who frequent these high-end restaurants. Everyone who enters and isn't already our client wins something. Why? Because we know that 70 percent of the people who try us become regular clients. Our fishbowls produce many winners and are another source of disguised discounts. Fishbowls have generated many high-end customers for us, and many of today's fully booked operators at John Robert's built practically their entire clientele from fishbowl winners.

Some people think we are a little aggressive in our marketing, meaning we give too much away. Let's look at it this way. Our choice could be to advertise or do one of our promotions that requires us giving away our initial services to gain more business.

We could take out a reasonably small ad in the paper that may cost us $1,000. The problem is that we can't control who is reading it. It may be a "right fit" potential customer or it may be someone who is not a "right fit." I want to ensure that my advertisement reaches only customers who fit into my target demographic and income level. Also, some customers may come in based on the promotion in the ad that you are offering, but find that you are not their type of place and never return.

Let's say an ad brings in 10 new customers, which I would consider very successful. These 10 people may come in and spend an average of $50, which would result in revenue of $500. Consider that a typical salon could pay their service providers in the range of 50 percent commission. Let's do the math: The ad cost us $1,000 and we got back $500; however, the cost of providing the service was $250 (commission to the service providers). In reality we are still out $750. We gained 10 new customers, who may or may not be the ones who prefer our type of salon; also, the typical retention on "blind" advertising is well below 40 percent.

In the second scenario, we give $50 gift certificates to a high-end Lexus dealership, restaurant, or travel agency to give to their top clients. Note that this is direct marketing to people who are our specific target, who definitely have high discretionary income. Let's say

10 of those people use their $50 gift certificates. First, we have no initial expense with this marketing. If 10 come in and use their $50, it ends up costing us $250. The 10 new customers received $500 in services, on which the service providers are paid 50%. Comparing the two scenarios, in advertising we incurred a $750 expense, while the gift certificate promotion cost us only $250, a savings of $500. Both promotions drew in 10 new customers, but I guarantee you our retention rate on Lexus drivers or high-end restaurant goers is substantially higher, about two times, than that from blind advertising.

## Stimulate Your Client's Mind

Many businesses have a great product and deliver the best service for an outstanding value, but if they let past customers forget that they exist they will miss huge opportunities.

All our marketing efforts are done with the thought of keeping our name in front of our existing clients. I call it "in-your-face marketing" or "repetitive awareness marketing." By using appropriate excuses to contact your clients constantly, you create not only a much more loyal customer, but also one who spends more of her discretionary income with your company. I think of it as stimulating the reticular activating system, the human brain's processing center to recall things the brain keeps in storage. The more you put your name in front of your customer, the more you stimulate his reticular activating system, and the less likely your name is to end up in his brain's attic.

At times we all use a company for some service and then forget that company when we need its service again. That's why it is imperative that we fight to stay in our customer's memory. The brain can keep only so much information current; the rest goes to the attic. Don't let your company be lost until next year's spring cleaning. I wish people had a birthday every month so we had an excuse to get in touch with them more often.

## Partner with Other Companies

One holiday season, in my search for win–win networking, I approached Jay Leitson, owner of Jayson's Pewter Mug, a restaurant in Beachwood,

Ohio. I told Jay I wanted to send each of our clients (7,000 at the time) a $15 gift certificate to his restaurant as a holiday gift. You should have seen his eyes light up—until I said I wanted these gift certificates at no charge. I explained that these gift certificates would go out to my clientele the week between Christmas and New Year's and would be valid for a specified and limited time, such as dinner only, Monday through Thursday, between January 1 and February 28. I further explained that the gift certificates would inform 7,000 upscale people of the existence of Jayson's Pewter Mug and give them the opportunity to try Jayson's during the slowest time of year. Almost every one of them would come with at least one other person, and all of them would spend a lot more than $15. With a little arm twisting, Jay agreed.

In mid-January, Jay called me and said, "I want to do this again. It was a huge success." During January and February our arrangement produced more than 1,300 new customers for Jayson's. They came with friends and spent an average of $85. In addition, they produced many bookings for Jayson's party room.

If the owner of Jayson's Pewter Mug had taken out a full-page advertisement in Cleveland's only daily newspaper, it would have cost him more than $10,000 and he could never have hoped to get 1,300 customers from it, especially during the slowest months of the year. This partnership was a home run. John Robert's clients got a gift certificate to a good restaurant, which they appreciated, and Jayson's Pewter Mug got 1,300 new clients from it. Win–Win.

## Adapting Our Ideas to Your Business

> It's not your customers' job to remember you.
> It's yours to make sure they never forget.
> —*Patricia Fripp*

Often, I hear people in other businesses say, "Well, that is a great idea, but it doesn't apply to my business. My business is different." For example, my neighbor Jeff works for a company that sells restaurant equipment. Jeff was a client of John Robert's long before we became neighbors, and he is always telling me, "I love John Robert's and all the things you do. I wish I could do stuff like that, but the hair salon business is different from the restaurant equipment business."

My response is: There is no difference at all. Forget about new customers, you probably have enough.

Make sure the clients are on a database and start to use that information.

This particular company sells espresso and cappuccino machines, bakery equipment, mixers, pastry sheets, cookie makers, ovens, and much more. However, the average customer was unaware of the variety of other products they sold.

The first thing Jeff should do after he sells a customer a cappuccino machine is to send him a thank you card. If the cappuccino machine was expensive, he should include a small gift. Then he should wait two or three weeks, and call him to ask him how the machine is working out. The customer may say, "Great, but I have one question. I know you told me this, but how do I do such-and-such?" He should take the time to tell him. He should be sure to let him know he shouldn't hesitate to call, even for the smallest thing.

Then Jeff should inform him of other things he sells that the customer may be interested in. This can be done by phone, in person, in an e-mail, or with a newsletter. In 6 months, Jeff should send him a notice reminding him of how to care for his cappuccino machine to keep it working efficiently and maintenance free. Jeff should tell the customer to contact him to schedule a time when he can come in and show the customer how to do this at no charge.

Jeff should find out what restaurant equipment he has. It doesn't matter that he bought it from someone else. Jeff should send him materials and reminders about how to care and maintain this equipment that he didn't even sell him. The next time the customer needs something, whom do you think he will call?

Jeff can also offer referral incentives and contests. He could send a $50 gift certificate to everyone who refers a new customer to him. He could send the gift certificate for every referral, and make it good toward the next order. Restaurant equipment isn't cheap, so the gift certificate ensures he will do business with Jeff again. Jeff has shown him that he appreciates him, and he has a $50 disguised discount.

Jeff could have a grand prize for the customer who refers the most people to him in 1 year. Announce the prize, then follow it up with a plug with details.

My message is this: Stop wasting your time on cold calls and start going deeper with your existing clients. As Henry Ford said, "Whether you think you can or you think you can't, you are probably right."

## A Memory Collector

I showed how my approach can be applied when I did a presentation for a photographers' association. The first thing I told them was, "I'm not going to pretend to know your business. I'm going to share many ideas that I have borrowed from other industries and that I implement successfully in my business. I'll leave it to you to decide how to tweak these ideas for success in your business." When I was done, I got a great reaction from the crowd.

As usual, one photographer came up to me on my way out and said, "I loved your ideas. I wish they applied to my business, but my business is different." I started telling him how he could benefit from increasing his customers' referrals by offering incentives and referral contests.

He said, "Yes, I can see that working, but digital cameras are killing the photography business. And besides, it's not like the hair business, where people need to come back every month. In our business, we do a wedding and we never see the couple again."

"Why is that? Why not contact them on their first anniversary, or when they start having children? Why wait for them to come back to you? You need to keep reminding them that you are their photographer."

I told him about the photographer at my wedding, Ron Kotar, of Studio K Photography, in Willoughby, Ohio. Ron has always reminded me that he isn't just a photographer; he is a memory collector. He captures the most important moments in people's lives and creates lasting memories for them. Similarly, we don't sell haircuts; we sell an experience.

Through newsletters and phone calls, Ron is always reminding me when it's time for an updated family portrait. At the end of every

September he sends a postcard to all clients reminding them of the dead-line for booking an appointment for a holiday portrait. Because of his ability to keep Studio K Photography in front of me and to make me aware of additional services he provides, I have used him countless times over the years, and not just for family photography. John Robert's has had Studio K photograph and videotape our grand openings, create slide shows, provide video footage for recruiting photo shoots, and videotape our services so we can display them in our waiting area to help us in-crease our clients' awareness of additional services we offer.

If Ron had not informed me and repeatedly kept his company's name if front of me, then I probably wouldn't have called him again after our wedding. Every year I meet clients who are photographers, and I'm sure I would have used one of them if Ron had not constantly reminded me that Studio K is the place I should go for all my photog-raphy and videography needs.

## Jewelry Stores
Different is not always better, but better is always different.

—Dale Dauten

Jewelry stores are among the first to find out about some very impor-tant events in people's lives. What if the jewelry store recorded this in-formation and used it to stimulate additional business with its existing customers? Revenue would increase dramatically. Most people go to a jewelry store for engagements, weddings, anniversaries, birthdays, and other significant occasions. The jeweler could record these dates and then congratulate the customer via mail, e-mail, or phone before an anniversary or birthday. As a service to the customer, a month before a couple's anniversary, the husband could receive a card saying, "I want to be the first to congratulate you on your fourth wedding anniversary, and I wish you many more. By the way, we have some outstanding diamond earrings on sale right now that would make a perfect anni-versary gift for your wife next month. If you wish, I can have them wrapped and sent to you at your office prior to June 25. Call me at your convenience, and we can make this anniversary extra-special."

If a jeweler did that for every anniversary, birthday, and any other special life event he was aware of, he would get more business from each of his customers. When customers need to buy jewelry, whose name would they think of first? In addition, the jeweler is providing more of a service, and he is generating an indebtedness by reminding the husband that an anniversary or birthday is just a month away.

## Florists

The same is true for many other businesses, including florists, who also know all the important dates and big events. Clifford's Flowers, a $5 million business in Quincy, Massachusetts, demonstrates how a small reminder can boost sales while keeping customers in the good graces of their wives and mothers-in-law. Clifford's Flowers uses sales records to generate letters reminding past customers to order for up-coming birthdays and anniversaries. How effective is this? The owner, James Clifford, has found that 75 to 85 percent of the customers who get the letter will reorder.

Whether it's a guilty conscience or Clifford's special incentives offered in these notices, customers send flowers to stay in the good graces of their mothers-in-law, wives, and other family members. Clifford's has not only increased sales dramatically but has also provided a great service that has enhanced a number of marriages and friendships. The bottom line is that three out of four customers say, "Yes, send my mother roses again." This clever combination of reminders and convenience makes it easy for past customers to become repeat customers, thus stimulating new sales.

## Retail Clothing Stores

I realized the impact of this service a few years ago, when Angela Huang called me a few days before my wife's birthday. Angela owns Windsware Boutique, in Moreland Hills, an upscale Cleveland suburb. My wife loves going to Windsware and buying clothes from Angela, but everything there is expensive. I cringe when I see shopping bags from Windsware Boutique because I know our bank account has taken a hit.

Angela called me and said, "John, I know it's Stacy's birthday on Thursday, and I know some things that she really, really likes. If you want, I could have them wrapped and delivered to your office." I realized that I had less than 48 hours before her birthday and that I still had to go and find something special. I also realized that I didn't have any time to be running around, and here was Angela offering to remove that whole burden from me. As much as I would have preferred to have spent less, it was an offer I couldn't resist. All this can be transformed into any business by managing a database based on annual or most recent purchases.

Based on my experience with Angela, I started thinking, "How can John Robert's offer this service to our clients?" One way we have duplicated this is by creating signage where people check out, telling them they can fill out a card that we will mail to their significant other before an event or holiday, saying "Suzanne would love to have. . . ." The client can check a few of the services listed, such as, "A facial and massage for Valentine's Day." It's similar to a bridal registry, except that it's for a spa.

A gift Stacy and I have always enjoyed receiving is a wine-of-the-month club: a different bottle each month, with the giver deciding the price range of wine and the number of months. We adopted that idea and started a spa-service-of-the-month. Each month the wife receives a different spa service: a facial, a pedicure, a massage, and so on. Husbands find this a great holiday gift because it lasts for an entire year.

## Don't Let Gift Certificates Expire

Many hotels, restaurants, and spas boast that as many as 50 percent of the gift certificates they sell are never redeemed, seeing that as money in the bank. I hold the opposite view: An unredeemed gift certificate is lost revenue from a potential lifetime client. So 30 days before the gift certificate expires, we contact the person holding it and say, "You may have forgotten about your John Robert's gift certificate." This has been very effective. I want to turn this person into a client who can spend $800 a year and who can refer two more people who will do the same. That's vastly better than saving $50 on an unused gift certificate.

## Keep Track of Customer Preferences

Amazon.com has mastered the art of utilizing customer preferences. If you are an Amazon customer, when you log onto the website, messages are waiting for you, such as "John, below is a list of books we think you would love, based on your purchase of *The Experience Economy.*" Another time, while riding in my friend Dave's car, I commented on how much I was enjoying the CD we were listening to. He said his father had purchased it for him. I said, "Your father doesn't seem to be the type to listen to this kind of music." Dave explained that his father had written down the titles of some of his CDs and had taken those titles to Amazon.com, which then gave him titles of several new CDs that Dave would probably like. Dave loved them, and because of this, he has been exposed to a wider range of music.

## Establish Frequent Buyer Programs

Bait the hook that suits the fish.

*—Dale Carnegie*

Frequent buyer programs are one of the strongest marketing ideas ever invented for creating repeat business and ultimately increased customer loyalty. But I see ways airlines could improve. Because I am a business owner who has to pay a significant amount of money to fly many of my employees all over the United States, I am dismayed that the airlines reward the traveler with frequent flier miles, not the purchaser. I see many programs for frequent fliers but none for frequent buyers. As a result, I have no loyalty to any one airline when I book flights for my staff. Instead I tell my travel agent to find me the most inexpensive flights. I know hundreds of other business owners who do exactly the same thing.

If an airline were to reward the purchaser with frequent flier miles, however, it would be a totally different situation. I would earn many thousands more miles a year and could use them toward both my own travel and employee travel. In that case, when I called my travel agent I would say, "I need five tickets to New Orleans, and be sure you book them on ABC Airlines, because I want the miles."

## Gain the Customer's Trust

One of the best marketers I have ever met is Ed Hollinshead, a mortgager. Stacy and I met Ed when we purchased our starter home in

1991. We found Ed extremely friendly and informed, but that alone wasn't what made him exceptional. He worked around our schedule; because Stacy and I both worked, he met us at our home in the evenings or on Sunday, whatever was best for us. Ed also reduced our anxiety as first-time homeowners as we went through the process of filling out paperwork, waiting for loan approval, and all the other steps involved, and did an excellent job of keeping us informed.

When the deal was finalized, I assumed we wouldn't need him for quite awhile, maybe 10, 15, or 20 years. Did we ever hear from him again? He became an excellent resource who contacted us about eight times a year. In addition to sending us quarterly newsletters, he sent us a postcard at every change of season with a list of seasonal activities to enjoy. In the summer, the card listed all the water and amusement parks, museums, and festivals, including dates, hours of operation, phone numbers, and addresses. In the winter, the card listed where we could see holiday lights, shop, and cut our own tree. His newsletters included referral incentives and information on how to care for our house. Everything he sent out, whether it was a newsletter, postcard, or magnet, had a note on it saying, "The highest compliment I could receive is a referral of a family member or friend."

What I liked most about Ed was his honesty. One time when interest rates dropped quite low, I called him to ask if we should refinance. His answer was no; he thought it wasn't cost effective for me yet, and he recommended I sit tight because he felt the rates would drop even lower. Mortgage lenders work on commission, and the only time they make money is when they sell a mortgage or refinance one. So what Ed told me was not the most advantageous thing for him in the short term; however, Ed thought only of the long term and what was in the best interest of his customers. Eventually, when he thought it was the most beneficial time to refinance, he called me, and I didn't hesitate to listen. I didn't compare rates; I just asked, "Where do I sign?"

Because of his honesty and the way he kept his name in front of us, not only did I refinance my mortgage and finance my new home with Ed, but I also eventually referred at least 20 people who purchased homes and used his services. His repetitive awareness marketing, reminding me that he was our lender and that he cared about us by providing small services, made us so much more loyal to him than we ever would have been to an ordinary mortgage lender.

## Educate the Customer About Your Services

Luck is preparation meeting opportunity.

*—Oprah Winfrey*

One day over lunch, my accountant, Jim Schulte, told me that although his business was going well, he knew it could be better. So we started brainstorming on how, instead of looking for new leads, he should try to go deeper with his existing customer base.

I learned he offered many services that I wasn't even aware of. At the time I was using him for quarterly profit-and-loss statements, year-end tax planning, and appraising salons we might acquire. I wasn't aware that he provided estate planning, employee bonus and profit-sharing strategies, and so much more. Just by talking with him along the right lines, I found out that he could help me through the muddle of all the different 401K plans that I had been bombarded with. I didn't have a clue about which to choose, and my accountant had experience with 401K plans, so I hired him to interview the companies and select the plan that best met my financial needs.

I told him, "I bet you have hundreds of clients who think of you only as their income-tax administrator and advisor." So we put together some programs to increase client awareness of all the services he provides. Quarterly newsletters and monthly e-mails give people some good advice and at the same time let them know that he is an expert in other areas. For instance, in December he now sends an e-mail that informs people of ways to reduce taxable income legally before the end of the year. He sends out other e-mails reminding people of upcoming deadlines for certain taxes owed and filing. Each time he also includes some expertise on additional services he provides. All this keeps his name in front of his clients and also provides them a service, giving them critical information that keeps them out of trouble with the IRS. All this ensures that the next time they need a service he provides, they will assuredly call him.

My accountant tells me his business with existing clients has increased nearly 30 percent during the first 12 months he has done this. He is now conducting a referral contest.

Attorneys would be just as successful using similar techniques within the restrictions on how they are allowed to solicit business. Attorneys could also send monthly updates on new laws that may impact your business, tips on ways to help you keep up on your legal inventory, and quarterly reminders that it's time again to take a look at this or that. Attorneys could make you aware that they are a resource for estate planning, lease negotiation, wills, real-estate transactions, employee agreements, policy handbooks, and anything else they provide. Quarterly newsletters and e-mails would be a fantastic tool that would accomplish all of this. The same is true for bankers and lenders. Each of these professionals would also be great resource when they refer you to other professionals for services. This significantly improves the loyalty factor. The more a business keeps its name in front of its clients, the greater the likelihood that the clients will use that business for additional services, especially if the clients receive value-added services such as updates and reminders.

## Nextel

Nextel does a great job of staying in front of its customers. Sometimes I become curious to see whether other companies have better cell phones and air-time rates than what I am paying. At that very moment, Nextel does something to remind me why I like to do business with them. Every time they come out with a new feature, they e-mail their customers via their cell phones. For instance, I am a big baseball fan, and I now have my phone set up to send me an e-mail alerting me that the Cleveland Indians game is about to start, and then to update the score after every run, and to send the final score as soon as the game ends. So if I cannot catch the game on radio or television, I always know the score. As another service, Nextel sends me an e-mail every morning telling me the weather forecast so I know what to wear.

I am sure other cell phones offer similar amenities, but Nextel's continuous in-your-face marketing, via e-mails and notices attached to their bill, prevents me from looking elsewhere.

Another brilliant strategy that cell phone companies use effectively is their promotion of accessories. Like many people, I enjoy all the latest gadgets, such as hands-free headset and wireless Internet. These companies know that the more accessories you buy, the more the company will get you to use their phone. Even more important, the more you invest in equipment and accessories, the less likely you are to switch to a different carrier.

## Insulate Your Customer from the Competition

By going deeper with your existing customers and personalizing their experiences, as well as continually demonstrating that you care and appreciate their business, you start to insulate them from competition and make it harder for other businesses to penetrate your relationship. Figures 5–1 and 5–2 demonstrate this example, using both John Robert's and an accounting firm as models.

The target diagram has three concentric circles: basic product and services; specialty products and services; and relationship. The interior circle, basic product and services, is the commodity portion of your business that people can get elsewhere. It may be what originally got them to try your business. In the John Robert's example, the basic layer includes hair and nail services and beauty products; for an ac-

**Figure 5–1. Insulating your customers from the competition: John Robert's.**

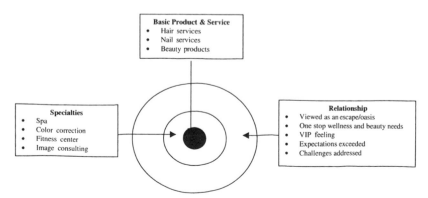

Basic Product & Service
- Hair services
- Nail services
- Beauty products

Specialties
- Spa
- Color correction
- Fitness center
- Image consulting

Relationship
- Viewed as an escape/oasis
- One stop wellness and beauty needs
- VIP feeling
- Expectations exceeded
- Challenges addressed

**Figure 5–2.  Insulating your customers from the competition: An accounting firm.**

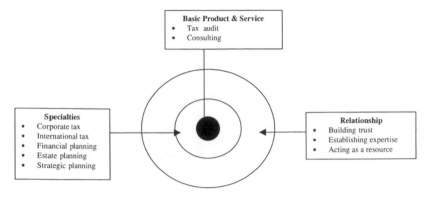

counting firm, it's tax audit and consulting services. Many businesses either offer only basic products or services or depend on this layer for the majority of their customers. This results in extremely low customer retention and loyalty.

The specialty layer starts to separate your business from the rest. At this level, new customers seek you out, especially because of your reputation in your area of expertise. For John Robert's, that may be services not found in their nearest salon, such as our spa services, fitness center, and specialized color correction. For an accounting firm, it could be services in corporate or international taxes or in financial and strategic planning. As businesses create and customers use services in this layer, customer retention and loyalty begin to increase.

The relationship layer is the point at which companies create a one-to-one relationship that totally separates that company from all its competition. In the process, the best companies insulate their customers from looking elsewhere, price shopping, getting quotes, and being enticed by advertising. At this level John Robert's and the accounting firm start to look very similar. This layer has less to do with technical services and more to do with the soft services that businesses sell. This layer becomes personal. It's no longer about what the business is selling; instead it's about creating and establishing a bond and a trust between business and customer. Once this layer is established, customers are more forgiving of any mistakes and price becomes irrelevant.

## Analyze Your Ideal Customer's Needs and Meet Them

> It takes the same amount of time to bait the hook
> for a big fish as it does for a small fish.
> —*Dale Carnegie*

I want to close this chapter on a subject that involves marketing but much, much more, as you will quickly see. I have used this as an exercise with my staff, as well as in salons where I consult. It always produces an "Aha" and drives decision-making as well. We pretend we have just purchased a fabulous machine that can mass produce as many new customers as we want. There are no limits; we can have anything we want. I ask:

What sex do you want this ideal customer to be?
What age range?
What is this customer's job and annual income?
What services and products will he or she purchase?
How often will this customer come in?
How much will this customer spend here in a year?

The answers I get are quite consistent, with very slight variations depending on the region where the salon is located:

Sex: female.
Age range: 25–45.
Job and income: a professional earning over $60,000 annually.
Services purchased: hair, color, nails, spa, and waxing.
Products purchased: everything we suggest.
Frequency of visit: at least once a week.
Amount spent in a year: At least $1,500.

At this point I say, "This is a pretty good client we would be making." Now I get the "Aha" when I continue:

"You say you want a professional female who makes at least $60,000 a year. When can she come in? What is she doing at 11:00 A.M. or

1:00 P.M.? Working—right? So when is she available?" You should see the looks on their faces.

They answer, "Evenings and weekends."

"Great. When are you available?"

Many say, "Well, I work Monday through Friday, 9:00 A.M. to 4:00 P.M." These are the same employees who complain in the break room, better known as the minimum-wage room, that their business is slow and they aren't getting enough ideal customers.

This is precisely why John Robert's is open from as early as 7:00 A.M. to as late as 10:00 P.M. and why we are open 7 days a week. (Our official hours are 9:00 A.M. to 8:00 P.M. Monday through Friday, and 8:00 A.M. to 5:00 P.M. Saturday and Sunday.)

My staff understands this. They know that just rearranging their hours will significantly increase their revenues. We track all our service providers' productivity, which is the amount of time they are booked per day. Some are booked 68 percent of the time, but when we dig deeper for the details, the picture changes dramatically. The 68 percent breaks down into bookings only 50 percent of weekdays and more than 90 percent of evenings and weekends; however, this person may be working only one evening and three weekdays. Just one change in staff scheduling, substituting an evening shift for a day shift, can dramatically increase the time booked, and because our staff is paid on commission, this has an impact on the paycheck.

As is true of just about every business today, we have many clients who are extremely busy. Many of them are business executives who can't plan far ahead and who want to get in when they can, usually evenings, weekends, or early mornings. It was our staff's, not management's, idea to open as early as 7:00 A.M. or stay open as late as 10:00 P.M. Our staff realized how much busier they were evenings and weekends, so they wanted to find a way to stretch those hours. The 7:00 A.M. idea was brilliant, because not only do we get many professionals who book appointments prior to their workday, but we also get many housewives who have a window of opportunity while the husband is at home getting ready for work and can watch the children.

It amazes me that so many businesses still have hours geared to the lifestyles their customers had 10, 20, or even 30 years ago. Whether a business is a grocery store or car dealership or anything else, the vast majority of its customers are couples who are both working and can shop only evenings. Doctors' offices, banks, travel agencies, government offices, utility companies, specialty retail stores, and many car dealerships still haven't adapted their hours to today's society. Many more businesses, including dry cleaners and car dealerships, could offer drop-off and pick-up services to the mutual advantage of the business and its customers. John Robert's worked out a deal with Marshall Ford, in Mayfield Heights. Every 3 months they pick up the cars of our employees who want the oil changed, do the service, and drop off the cars. We don't care on what day this is done, so Marshall Ford can turn a slow day into a very profitable one by doing an additional 40 oil changes.

## Hobby Shops

Many businesses operate for their convenience, not for their customers'. When my son Johnni wanted a complete set of baseball cards, I thought first of a memorabilia shop near our house. After I dropped Johnni off at school, I drove past this shop, about 9:15 A.M., and saw that it was closed. A few days later, I got off work early, drove there at 5:30 P.M., and saw the closed sign again. I got out of my car to read their hours: Monday through Friday 11:00 A.M. to 5:00 P.M., and Saturday by appointment. The man who owns the memorabilia shop complains constantly about how bad business is and how he doesn't make enough money, though it shouldn't be surprising.

**Ways to be a rainmaker**
- Institute a referral contest that enrolls and entices your customers to work for you as your sales force.
- Focus on the retention rates of keeping the top 10% of your best customers.
- Go deeper with your top clients by showing them how much you appreciate them. Reward them with things that will make them more loyal and at the same time do more business with you.
- Figure how even a 5% increase in your customers average ticket can have a huge impact on your bottom line, then think of every opportunity your staff has to increase it.

- Constantly brainstorm how you can raise the bar on your Secret Service systems, especially with your VIPs.
- Figure what your customers' lifetime value is and make sure your team understands that significance.
- Avoid public discounting, but instead utilize disguised techniques.
- Network/partner with other reputable businesses that share similar customer bases.
- Create positive excuses to keep your name in front of your customer, for example, happy birthday, anniversary, and so on.
- Keep track of and manage customer preferences.
- Establish frequent buyers programs.
- Insulate your customer from the competition.
- Analyze your customer's needs and exceed the ways you meet them.

# CHAPTER 6

# Creating Passionate Team Members:

## Developing a Strong Corporate Culture

> Take my building, equipment, all my money, my land, but leave me my people, and in one year I will be on top again.
>
> —*Andrew Carnegie*

In Chapter 5 I discussed how one of the best marketing techniques you can have is a happy client. The only better marketing technique is to have happy employees.

The one common theme among the most successful companies is that they take good care of their employees and create a strong corporate culture. If you treat your team members well, the majority of them will take good care of your clients. A strong corporate culture is a company's best competitive advantage, and it's probably the most difficult quality to replicate.

John Robert's corporate mission statement says we want all our long-term employees to regard their decision to work with us as one of the best decisions they ever made. We strive to make these words come true. If we succeed with just 25 percent of our employees, we take pride in making that many people feel that good about working somewhere.

Our senior team members created our core values, which we teach to all our employees on their orientation day. We value our:

1. Team
2. Guests
3. Community
4. Sustainability.

## Encourage Teamwork

Your team members are as high a priority as our guests, maybe even higher. If you find some great employees who understand the true meaning of a team, you don't have to worry about how well they will take care of your guests. Teach this from day one and reinforce it every day in various ways.

Here are 10 guidelines that are of paramount importance in managing staff:

1. You cannot expect 100 percent of your staff to become ideal employees.
2. You can expect that 5 percent of your staff will be naturals at living the mission.
3. The secret to succeeding is not to dismiss the employees who don't fit your ideal model, but to mold them, to find out which buttons to push, what hat to wear to motivate them. You may fail with some, but you will succeed with many others, and your success will be well worth it.
4. Development of your staff is your responsibility. Leadership is motivating people to reach their highest potential. People like to generalize that nobody wants to work anymore, and the younger generation has poor work ethics and is useless. If you believe that and your business is dependent on employees, you might as well close your doors.
5. Nobody rises to low expectations.
6. There is a winner in everyone.

7. Many successful people were bad employees at one time. At some point in their careers, someone knew what to do to motivate them.
8. Keeping up morale is dependent on the boss.
9. No successful business owner has continuous bad luck with employees.
10. For the most part, the people we hire do not possess any more winning qualities than the people who work elsewhere. We just do a very good job at bringing out their winning qualities.

## Reduce Turnover

There is no such thing as a labor shortage, just a turnover crisis. Turnover is usually more responsible for understaffing than are growth and expansion. The best of the best not only have programs and people in place committed to constant recruitment and utilizing excellent hiring techniques, but are also dedicated to a strong corporate culture to reduce turnover.

Secret Service systems are as essential for your employees as for your clients. You must train all your support staff—your managers and administrative teams—that their customers are your team members. The people in John Robert's corporate office know this better than anyone else. Melissa Voinovich, our People Development Coordinator, and Mary Iacobucci, our Payroll Administrator, get dozens of questions every week about payroll and policy. These women are excellent at providing our employees with unforgettable customer service. They respond quickly and efficiently, never act as if any question is foolish, and serve as a reliable resource for the rest of the staff, even if it goes far beyond their job descriptions, such as helping an employee deal with a bill collector. Melissa has created systems, checklists, and reminders to make sure we deliver and exceed our employees' expectations. Lisa Adams, our Spa Director, and Eric Hammond, our Director of Operations, have often gone well above and beyond for their team members, including being on the phone with them until the wee hours or accompanying them to professional counseling.

The John Robert's culture starts when an employee is hired. Because we have more than 120 employees in three locations, it's increasingly difficult to help newer team members break the ice and get acquainted with as many team members as possible. One day I walked into the manager's office at our Mayfield salon. I found a young woman who I assumed was a client who had made a wrong turn.

"May I help you?" I asked.

"Eric [the manager] sent me in here to get a stapler."

"Do you work here?"

"Yes, do you?"

At that point I realized we were growing a little faster than I'd like. Growth is good, but we needed to improve our staff's awareness of new hires. We start training our employees in the recruitment and interview process, through orientation and their first 90 days, and continue communicating our company's vision and direction.

## Refine the Employee Experience Cycle

You may own the business, but you just rent the people.

—Jack Welch

As with the Customer Experience Cycle, every company has an Employee Experience Cycle whether or not the company realizes it. Employees will experience first impressions about the company and the company's image during the interview, after they are hired, during their first six months, and so on.

Again, as with the Customer Experience Cycle, most Employee Experience Cycles happen by accident rather than by design. By consciously creating an Employee Experience Cycle, you can be proactive and can prevent situations that typically reduce employee morale.

Whenever you lose an employee, try to look at your Employee Experience Cycle to see what you may have missed. Concentrating on this cycle will help you deal with patterns and trends that constantly repeat themselves.

For example, nearly every new employee at John Robert's starts off thinking that this has to be one of the most fun places to work. But within two weeks, they realize that it's hard work. Because they are new, they are learning everything for the first time, constantly asking questions, and are inundated with information.

Knowing this, we meet with them about two weeks after they have been hired, tell them how well we think they are doing, how impressed everyone is with them, and how we can already tell they are going to be a big part of our future success. Something that simple can prevent their becoming so overwhelmed that one day they just come in and quit.

Develop systems that help your new employees feel comfortable right away. First, as soon as they have been hired, send a card congratulating them on joining your team. Many companies celebrate an employee's retirement, but forget to celebrate her hiring. In the employee lounge put up a banner showing the new team member's picture, name, and position. That way the rest of the staff can greet her by name the first time they see her. At John Robert's, the Human Resource Coordinator sends everyone a voice mail about the new hire and puts her picture and bio in all the paychecks. As a manager I don't have to worry about seeing a staff person I don't know in my office.

Just as you should focus on every aspect of the Client Experience Cycle, also take the time to really look at the Employee Experience Cycle. To help you get started, here is a part of the John Robert's Employee Experience Cycle.

# Employee Experience Cycle
## *The First Interview*
- The candidate has heard of John Robert's through one or more of the following:
  - Our recruiting strategies.
  - From an existing John Robert's client.
  - Is referred by someone who is working at John Robert's.
  - Is a client.
- The candidate fills out an application.

- The candidate is contacted within 72 hours and the first interview is scheduled.
- The first interview covers non-negotiable aspects of our employment:
    - Pay
    - Attendance
    - Transportation
    - Attitude
    - Community involvement
    - Continual advanced education.
- The candidate is given a tour of the salon.
- The candidate shares aspirations and learns about John Robert's culture, core values, and expectations.
- The candidate is asked questions that reveal whether his or her disposition is positive or negative.
- If the fit is right, the candidate is scheduled to come back for an observation day when the salon is busy.
- If at any time a candidate is determined not to be a right fit, we send a thank you card and end the application process.

## The Second Interview

- On observation day (second interview), the candidate is introduced to as many team members as possible, including the potential team leader.
- Candidate is given someone to shadow and left to roam freely and interact with as many team members as possible for as long as desired (on the floor, in the break room, etc.). Asking questions is strongly encouraged.

## The Third Interview

- The candidate is then called to schedule a third and final interview.
- Mutual expectations are discussed, as are any possible concerns that may have come from the previous first two interviews.
- The candidate is hired.
- The candidate receives a congratulatory card within 24 hours of being hired.

## Orientation

- On the first day the new hire learns the history of John Robert's, accomplishments, awards won, legacy, core values, and company policies.
- On the second day the new hire attends an interactive hands-on class that introduces all the Secret Service systems that the new hire will be expected to learn and follow.
- The new hire meets several key members of the management team.
- The new hire is given a John Robert's History Portfolio to take home and review.
- The new hire takes a legacy test to see how much she retained about the John Robert's history.

## The First 90 Days

- A large banner is displayed in the employee lounge with the new team member's picture, name, and position.
- A company-wide voice mail is sent introducing our newest team member.
- All new employee pictures, names, and positions are announced in the monthly team newsletter.
- All new employees are introduced at monthly company meetings.
- At 15, 30, 60, and 90 days the new employee and her manager meet to ensure that mutual expectations are being met. The new employee also receives different services to understand what a guest experiences.
- The new hire sets goals to be achieved in her first year.

## The Ongoing Experience

- All employees have to meet the minimum yearly requirement for advanced education hours.
- Multiple managers send *Caught You Doing Something Right* cards to employee.
- The employee has an opportunity to win the Employee of the Month award at a monthly meeting.
- Any and all accomplishments are celebrated via monthly meetings, team newsletters, company voice mails, and so forth.

- The employee has the opportunity to be promoted, which is celebrated at the restaurant of her choice.
- Employee achievements are recognized at the annual *Johnni's* Awards Celebration.
- All team members attend an annual summit at which top presenters are featured.
- Team members have the opportunity to apply for The John Robert's Leadership Development Program.
- Service providers have the opportunity to join the John Robert's Design Team, which conducts fashion shows and performs makeovers on television.
- At their 5-year anniversary employees get a room named after them, marked with a plaque. They also receive an amethyst necklace.

Take the time to write out the Employee Experience Cycle for your company. Don't forget to ask your employees what their personal experiences were. Their input is essential to discovering difficult periods at which an employee might need extra support.

## Boost Morale

Nobody rises to low expectations.

*—Carl Boyd*

Find a way to celebrate everything including the small accomplishments. At John Robert's one of our most effective tools in boosting morale is our "Caught You Doing Something Right" cards. We keep stacks of these cards in the employee lounge, call center, dispensary, and any other room a team member enters. We started using these cards as a management tool, and now the entire company uses them. An employee may open his drawer and find a "Caught You Doing Something Right" card thanking him for helping someone through a mini-crisis the day before. Most employees save these cards indefinitely.

Our management team is required to catch people doing something right on a regular basis. It has become so routine that we now have a spreadsheet with every employee's name down one side and each manager's name across the top. The manager fills in the date he or she last sent that employee a "Caught You Doing Something Right" card. This way we can spot when someone hasn't been recognized in a while and immediately catch them.

We have held "Caught You Doing Something Right" contests, and the employee who gives the most cards wins a gift certificate to a nice restaurant. The entire team really gets into it. One shy manicurist went home one night and wrote out 111 personalized cards to everyone on our staff.

At John Roberts, we believe morale is so important that we track each manager's effort to boost morale on a weekly basis. Managers must fill out a leadership-tracking sheet which includes the question, "What have you done to improve morale?" They continually must think of creative ways to recognize people, catch them doing things right, and show them how much we appreciate them.

## Recognize Employees' Performance

What gets recognized gets repeated.

—*Lou Holtz*

I learned this lesson in grade school. I was not an outstanding student, to say the least. On top of that I was not well behaved. One time my mother came home from a parent–teacher conference very upset with me after hearing all my teachers say what a terror I was at school. One teacher, trying to be kind, finally said, "John always looks nice." That was a stretch. My clothes were second hand, and when I look at my school pictures, I think I never combed my hair. However, this one positive thing the teacher said made me feel so good that from that day forward (even though my grades didn't improve and I was still constantly in the principal's office) I started taking the time to be as well dressed and groomed as possible, because someone made me feel good about it.

Every week at John Robert's we post a "Beat the Week" in the employee lounge, which displays each employee's best week ever. If a designer has her best week ever, she wins a free lunch as well as earning her best paycheck ever.

Our staff is so motivated that they start tracking their sales as early as Tuesday to see if they are on pace to beat their best week ever. When they sense they could possibly do it, they do just about anything they can. They tell the call center to book them more appointments, and they decide to come in an hour earlier or stay later to accommodate clients.

John Robert's makes a big deal out of it when a service provider hits certain milestones for the first time, such as $1,000, $2,000, $3,000, and $4,000 in service sales in a week. For nail technicians, a great week is $1,500 in sales.

Denise Florjancic, one of our top nail technicians, got so tired of seeing only designers beat $2,000 that she went on a mission to break $2,000. No manicurist in our salon had ever come close to that number, so many people thought she was crazy. She had to average $400 a day, which doesn't happen even on a Saturday, the busiest day.

A few times Denise got close by coming in early and staying late. Then one week she made $404 on Tuesday, $410 on Wednesday, and $402 on Thursday. Now all she had left was Friday and Saturday, her two busiest days, and she needed less than $784. Everyone started to get excited. On Friday she hit $411. Now she was only $373 away. We looked at her Saturday appointments and figured she could easily break $400. She was actually going to do it.

The first thing on Saturday morning, three of Denise's afternoon appointments canceled, which meant she wasn't going to make it. She was crushed, but the entire team started promoting her to all their clients. Another manicurist, Jennifer, saw that she had a "no request" appointment, a client who had not requested anyone specific, and had the front desk give her to Denise. When the day was over, with the help of the entire team, an exhausted Denise finished the week with $2,002 in sales. We popped champagne and celebrated.

The "Beat the Week" contest can be a strong incentive tool for management to use. One Friday a client called imploring us to get her in the next day for a blow-dry style because she had an important event Saturday evening. Everyone was booked solid, but because she was such a good client, I asked a designer to open an hour earlier to accommodate her. The problem was that this particular designer always found an excuse why she couldn't do anything extra, and if you got her to agree, she moaned about it until you regretted asking her. I saw that she could possibly beat her week if she had a great Saturday. With the extra incentive of beating her week and winning a prize, she enthusiastically accepted the earlier appointment.

## Increase Employee Retention

A business's employee retention rate is every bit as critical as its customer retention rate.

We hold our black-tie event for our entire team, our Johnni's (see Chapter 2), in February, in the middle of our slow season. The event invigorates our staff at a time when it's greatly needed. We hold Employee Appreciation Month in May. During this time the management team washes all the team members' cars, has surprise parties, treats the team to a cookout during work hours, and even gives one lucky employee limousine service to and from work for a day (the winner is usually the person who lives the farthest away). We also designate six different weeks per year as department appreciation weeks for individual departments and create an awareness campaign to demonstrate how important they are to our organization. We schedule these weeks to coincide with company-wide meetings so we can celebrate and recognize that department in front of everyone.

At one of our manager retreats, everyone talked about wanting personalized John Robert's license plates. We decided the company would pay for them and that we would offer them to the entire team. To my amazement, more than 40 employees signed up. They got plates with JR Spa, JR Nails, JR Hair, and so on. We also purchased license-plate frames with "John Robert's Hair Studio & Spa" and our phone number. The best part of this is that I am fairly certain these 40 employees are not out looking for a new job.

We provide an Instructor Appreciation night annually that invites the area cosmetology instructors to experience our spa at our expense. We do this for three reasons. The first is that we want the instructors to know how much we appreciate the role they play in our industry; second, we want the instructors to experience the latest and greatest in

salons and spas so they would be better at what they are teaching; and
third, we want the instructors to encourage their best students to come
to work at John Robert's.

John Robert's is still a small company, which sometimes makes it difficult to compete with all the benefits that large companies can offer,
some of which have very generous amenities on site for employees. We
had to be creative. For example, we now offer, at no cost to John Robert's,
a drop off and pick up dry cleaning service twice a week for all our employees, eliminating a chore employees would have to do on a day off. We
were also able to negotiate a volume discount with the dry cleaner.

## Treat Staff Like Your Best Customers

To give first-class service, you must first receive it.

Every staff member at John Robert's who is promoted gets to
choose where she wants her boss to treat her to dinner. Although this
in itself is a great reward, it also lets our staff see how much they enjoy
being treated like royalty by a five-star restaurant. It makes them more
aware of the attention to detail that goes into excellent customer service. Our intention is for them to take that experience and incorporate
it into their approach toward our guests.

Every employee gets a paid day off on her birthday, as well as a full
day of pampering at John Robert's that includes a facial, massage,
pedicure, manicure, haircut, and lunch. Employees love being able to
experience what it feels like to be a client, and they see and hear everything from a new perspective. For instance, they can appreciate how
the client interprets a staff conversation, or they may observe something that clients see but that employees usually don't notice. For instance, lying on a massage table and staring at the ceiling, an employee
may see that nobody has cleaned the heating vent in awhile. Our
birthday days of pampering have helped open many employees' eyes to
their need to give attention to detail as a service provider.

## Create Passion in the Workplace

Create passionate team members, and they will produce passionate
customers.

We make a point of teaching new staff that John Robert's is all about the experience, the essence of the service. Denise Thompson, our Marketing Director, describes this very well: "As part of this, our management team teaches a service class that includes a number of exercises. One of the exercises is going out to lunch and observing the service at the restaurant. After discussing different aspects of service all morning, it's an awakening for our new staff to pay attention to the service around them. We discuss what met or exceeded their expectations, what opportunities exist for improvement, and how different roles have an effect on fellow team members. The class participants begin to see the systems that are in place and their benefits. Now it's much easier for them to see and understand our systems, and why we have them. The more chances they have to experience service, good or bad, the more they learn and understand. When they experience great service, they begin to uncover and appreciate the secret service systems those establishments have in place. They even think of ways to duplicate them in our own industry. The only difficulty is that experiencing great service is like drinking good wine: once you have tasted the finer reserves, you can't go back to the $10 bottles."

Another way we recognize our employees is through our room-naming ceremony. Several of our employees have been with us longer than five years, a big accomplishment in our industry. We started the tradition of naming a room after any employee who has been with us five years. A nice plaque at the doorway displays the name, and we hold a ceremony during which the recipient slides her nameplate into the frame.

The main salon, spa, and call center are all named after someone. People constantly ask me, "What will you do when you run out of rooms?" I respond, "If we have that many people hitting five years, then we probably will be able to open more salons, which means we will have a lot more doors to dedicate."

## Southwest Airlines

Southwest Airlines is a case study in creating passion among the ranks. Their philosophy is "Hire for attitude and train for skill." More than anything else, they look for people who are fun, with a special kind of spirit, and then train them. At Southwest, everything comes from the top. Tom Kelleher, the founder and CEO, sets the tone for the whole company with his great sense of humor and ability to show the employees how much he cares about them. He always stands up for them first, and conveys they take priority over customers. By treating the employees with so much respect and warmth, they do the same for each other and the customers. They make living legends out of their service heroes. They celebrate every accomplishment, even the smallest ones, in the biggest ways. They show people what legendary service looks like, then trust them to do the right thing. They make it a practice to give everyone—customers, co-workers, friends, and family— more than they expect. Instead of loving techniques and using people, they love the people and use the techniques. This "love theory" carries over into their community involvement as well. They let love be the motivator, and take part in volunteer activities for the greater good, at the same time becoming better for it.

## Give an Excellent Orientation Program

We don't hire people with more winning qualities than anyone else; we just bring out their winning qualities.

Do you think Walt Disney World in Florida has been lucky enough to find 60,000 perfect employees? This is unlikely. The company has taken on the goal of making its employees perfect. Borrowing ideas from companies such as Walt Disney World, we have found that an effective way to get our new employees involved is through our orientation program.

We teach them the history of John Robert's: how we started, where we came from, what it took to get here, everything that happened along the way, and where we are going. New employees also receive a history portfolio that has every article we have ever been in, pictures of every stage of our salons and expansions, awards we have won, and letters from clients and politicians. Our new employees share this portfolio with family and friends.

At the end of orientation, we give a Legacy Test to see how much knowledge about John Robert's has been retained. We don't grade this test; it's just a review. We ask questions such as, "Of the fifteen awards listed below, which has John Robert's won?" To employees' amazement, the correct answer is fourteen out of fifteen. Another question is, "Of the twenty-four community projects listed below, what has John Robert's been involved in?" Again, the answer is twenty-three out of twenty-four.

When we finish reviewing the test, the employees are also amazed at how much they just learned about John Robert's. They talk about these things with clients the next day when they give their first shampoo. We arm our new employees with so much ammunition and pride about John Robert's that they want to brag about it.

## Starbucks

Starbucks goes through extensive efforts to not only select great employee candidates, but also to train them to be successful in their new careers. The first interview with Starbucks consists mostly of answering questions, and this determines whether the applicant is called back for a second one. If the applicant passes the second interview, he comes in to fill out a great deal of paperwork and read about the company and its expectations. New hires are given a "Learning Journal Guide," and take classes at the Starbucks center on Simply Service, Communicating Coffee, and the Starbucks Experience before they begin to work in the store. The classes include learning their mission, history, and Starbucks skills (such as enhancing, listening and acknowledging, building self-esteem, and asking for help).

Each employee is given many books and binders to read and goes through about 80 hours of education and the Learning Journal Guide, core 1 and core 2. It includes selling both merchandise and an experience. The training stresses that Starbucks should be a third place for people. The first place is the person's home and the second is work. Your third place should be one where you can relax.

Expectations of employees include acknowledging new service, recognizing each other, treating each other with respect, contributing to the experience, and expressing enthusiasm.

Employees are reviewed every 6 months, and individual development plans are discussed. Employees are evaluated on the first impressions they project and their skills. If an employee is late or performs below standard he or she is written up, and after three write-ups is put on probation.

Starbucks has service standards as well. Espresso shots should take 18 to 23 seconds. Milk must be frothed fresh each time at 160 degrees F. All recipes must be followed consistently. They constantly have secret shoppers who check that all service standards are being met. They also have a "Just say yes" philosophy, no matter what. Free drink coupons may be given, even if the customer accidentally ordered the wrong beverage. Employees are timed and judged on their use of acknowledgment and customers' names.

Continuing education includes classes before the holidays to learn about new merchandise, and so forth.

## Retain or Retrain

Retaining existing employees far outweighs retraining brand new ones. Your business is your people, and you have to put them first, even if that means putting them before profits. Putting staff first includes involving them in decisions typically viewed as managerial. There are many critical decisions that need to be made by management because it is in the best interest of the entire organization. When a policy or decision can affect the morale of the entire staff, however, it is imperative to have their involvement and include them in the solution, which it is hoped will benefit everyone. For example, John Robert's Mayfield location is open seven days a week. With customers working so many hours and having less free time during the week, there's a huge demand for salon and spa services on Sundays. Also, many of our clients enjoy coming in on Sunday, especially during the winter when their husbands watch football all day. At 8:00 A.M. on a Sunday, our appointment book can appear empty, but by 10:00 A.M. the rest of the day is booked solid because many people find they have some spare time and call to see what we have available. Very few salons in our area are open on Sunday.

From the viewpoint of our employees, our staff has increased so much that we have more hairdressers than hair stations. We have to stagger shifts and days worked so that our employees can get all their hours. Many salons use this concept of double-shifting, or having many more designers than stations. Double-shifting helps maximize space and overhead without expanding or building multiple locations.

Seniority determines who works Sundays, so newer operators work Sundays until they build up a clientele. Even though it's their busiest day, most operators dislike working Sundays. It was always hair designers' top complaint on their reviews; if they didn't have to work Sundays, they would be totally happy. I can understand that. Sunday is a family day, and working it means missing out on a lot of family events.

We faced a real dilemma: stay open on Sundays and risk hurting employee morale, or close on Sundays, lose a large amount of revenue, and face the need to expand sooner than we would like. We generate $5,000 to $7,000 on a Sunday, and that's with a small staff on hand. Also, Sunday business is different. If we were to close on Mondays, most of that business would probably trickle to the rest of the week. But Sunday clients typically cannot come in on a different day, and if we were closed on Sunday, they would go elsewhere or forgo the services.

In addition to the potential loss of revenue, we couldn't give our designers eight hours during the week to replace the Sunday hours. We also had several apprentices about to graduate onto the floor, and we needed to find 40 hours worth of available stations to accommodate each of them.

So closing on Sundays would mean either having to expand at Mayfield or opening a new location. Both options were impossible: we couldn't expand at Mayfield because no more space was available, and we couldn't open a new location because we had just opened a salon in Solon, a huge investment.

We decided the staff would vote to decide whether to close on Sundays. As the staff discussed the issue, they started saying, "Wait. I don't know if I want to close on Sundays. That's my biggest day. I can't afford to not work any Sundays." The staff actually started to panic. "You can't close Sundays. Whatever you do, don't close Sundays." By the time it came to a vote, nobody wanted to close Sundays, about a third wanted to continue working Sundays, and the rest wanted to rotate Sundays. In the end everyone was much happier because we gave them a choice, and while they were deciding, they realized how important Sundays actually are.

It's important to view turnover in a positive way and to try to ensure that people leave with a good feeling about your company. Former employees will come in contact with many of your current and potential clients, and many of your former employees will also turn into good clients.

So make sure you have Secret Service systems in place for former employees. Send them cards when they leave, saying how much you appreciate the time they worked for you and how you wish them much luck in the future. If the person worked for you for several years, send flowers to the home. When possible, recognize the individual at the last company meeting he attends or in a newsletter. Continue to send birthday cards and holiday cards.

To help us always have a constant influx of good employment candidates, we offer our staff a cash incentive for referring people to work for us; we likewise offer our guests a $50 or $100 gift certificate if they refer someone to work for John Robert's.

## Encourage Going Above and Beyond

The most difficult systems to implement are ways for employees to go above and beyond. You cannot always anticipate opportunities for an employee to go above and beyond; you can only create a culture that fosters that kind of creative thinking.

To create employees who are the best, the best companies find good people and enroll them into a culture of legendary customer service. This is done through constant awareness campaigns and training from the moment of hiring.

For instance, unforgettable customer service is the focus of our orientation. Each new employee takes a "Secret Service" class in which we cover all our Secret Service systems and share our legacy stories of how people constantly go above and beyond for our customers. This typically creates an awareness of high standards and the desire to measure up to them and eventually to be included in the legacy stories told. Follow up a great orientation with recognition of superior service in meetings, voicemails, cards, awards, and newsletters.

Though you may not be able to create a specific system to ensure that your employees go above and beyond for your clients, employees are constantly reminded that exceptional customer service is what you are all about.

When problems arise with an employee, an employer has to decide whether to invest time and effort in making that employee successful. Make that decision on the basis of whether the employee shows enthusiasm and passion. One of your goals as management is to make certain every employee has, at the very least, enthusiasm. Passion is even better.

Enthusiastic employees like where they work, they like the work they do, and they do it very well. You may have many good employees who are very enthusiastic about what they do but who may not be passionate. They do a great job for you and your clients, but helping your company become the best of the best is not one of their major concerns. These people still have enormous value.

If an employee cannot be consistently enthusiastic, and you have exhausted every effort toward that goal, then cut your losses and terminate the relationship. An employee who has a difficult time being enthusiastic about the job and company is probably influencing other employees, and it's critical that you catch the situation before others are infected.

By contrast, an employee with passion is someone whose ambitions are in sync with the company's ambitions. Many passionate people gravitate to leadership roles in their companies.

I recently came across a newsletter produced by the Garick Corporation (www.garick.com) that emphasized how passion makes the difference. It shared some startling facts: 50 percent of all CEOs of Fortune 500 companies had a C or C minus average in college. Nearly 75 percent of all U.S. presidents were in the bottom half of the class. More than 50 percent of all millionaire entrepreneurs never finished college. What makes it possible for people who might seem ordinary to achieve great things? Passion. Nothing can take the place of passion and what it can do for you as a leader.

# How the Big Companies Do It

Success leaves clues.

*—John Stanton*

Many of the ideas we have implemented were inspired by great companies such as Progressive Auto Insurance and MBNA Bank. Even though we can only dream of duplicating many of the amenities they can provide, we can be creative by tweaking them and adding them to our benefits portfolio.

## Progressive Auto Insurance

Progressive Auto Insurance, headquartered in Mayfield Village, Ohio, is known for being open 24 hours a day and for giving consumers Progressive's quote for auto insurance as well as the quotes of three other leading companies. It's easy to see why Progressive has become one of the top auto insurance companies in the United States.

What is less well known is how well Progressive takes care of its internal customers; its employees. Progressive employees are treated to on-site dry cleaning, a fitness facility, travel services, and massages, to name just a few benefits. Progressive bears part of the cost of special benefits such as fitness memberships and massages. There's an on-site health care center where employees can have blood drawn, throat cultures done, and prescriptions filled. Progressive also offers tuition reimbursement, flex time, casual dress, profit sharing, and subsidized child care. In addition, Progressive has negotiated discounts for its employees at local malls, auto stores, salons and spas, cell phone companies, computer stores, amusement parks, florists, home improvement stores, and professional sporting events. Why would you want to work anywhere else?

Many of these discounts and amenities are actually not beyond the reach of small and mid-size businesses. The fact is that many companies would appreciate the opportunity to offer these services and discounts to your employees.

## MBNA Bank

MBNA Bank, a credit card company headquartered in Wilmington, Delaware, has been chosen as one of the top 100 U.S. companies to work for by *Fortune Magazine.* It's easy to see why. MBNA offers its employees aerobic classes, fitness centers, intramural sports, and cafes that offer both healthful meals and catering. In-house shops feature gift items, magazines, dry cleaning, photo-processing, flowers, shoe repair, and postal services. MBNA offers scholarships for children, in-house day care, financial assistance with adoption, paid leave for parents of newborns, financial advisors, and tuition reimbursement. Add to all that bonuses for employee ideas that are implemented, limousine transportation, and an extra week of vacation if you get married or if a grandchild is born.

Every door in every MBNA building posts this message: "Think of yourself as the customer."

## Create Opportunities for Employees to Learn from One Another

Once a month we hold a 3-hour meeting for our entire company. As part of the agenda, two or three successful employees share their stories about where they began and what it took to get where they are today. These stories are inspirational to newer staff members who may be struggling and lacking confidence. It may seem that the top performers were born with the skills they possess today, but to the surprise of many staff, nearly every one of our top performers struggled, sometimes miserably, when she started and almost quit because she thought she could never make it.

At one meeting, a facialist told her story. I thought she would be inspirational, because although she now has a large clientele, she too struggled when she started at John Robert's. She had started as an assistant to our hairdressers but disliked the job, which was too fast-paced for her. She was thinking about quitting and looking for another career when we realized that her very nurturing and pampering style would be ideal for our spa. It is a totally different environment: relaxing, nurturing, quiet, and slower paced. Here she immediately excelled.

I was surprised because she told a very different story. She started with how unhappy her childhood had been. She spoke about an abusive father who destroyed any self-esteem she had. Life got so bad that she became anorexic. Around that time, when she had a blind date and needed her hair done, she came into John Robert's for the first time and I did her hair. I told her how incredible she would be in our industry, and that she should consider cosmetology school and someday coming to work for us. Excited, she went home that day and told her mother about a salon owner who saw something in her and believed in her. She signed up for beauty school, graduated, and the rest is history. Fortunately for her and John Robert's, she was treated well and made to feel special. We are very fortunate to have this woman.

The most important thing about our industry is that we physically touch so many clients, and are probably the only industry to do this in such a positive way that they look forward to it. We can transform their exterior looks and make them feel great about themselves instantly.

We never know what a client is going through. We see more than 250 clients a day, and at least three of them probably have some very serious concerns in their lives. Many people never share these things with us, but they need to escape for a short time, from 30 minutes to 3 hours. That's why we need to be on our "A" game every time, every day.

### GOING ABOVE AND BEYOND

Denise Thompson, Marketing Director: "Of our four core values, the first and most important is team. Our team is the most valuable asset we have, and we team members are always respected as such. Our team is our strength. We believe in each other and trust the systems which have made us successful. We are fortunate to have owners who believe in us and help us to be the best we can be. When I joined John Robert's, I had just received my esthetic license. John DiJulius allowed me to begin a new position with no experience and provided me with the additional training I needed to be successful. When I was ready for a new challenge, John was looking for a manager. Again, he was willing to give me a chance at new responsibilities and to provide the support and the foundation

I needed. Now, three years later, I cannot believe how much I have grown. I went from not knowing how to turn on a computer to creating reports and presentations and consulting with other salons. All our people receive the training and support they need to be successful.

It's my belief that people need to experience good service in order to provide it. As a director, I know I must provide the same excellent service to our team members that we expect them to provide our guests. This includes showing genuine care and concern for their needs. Because we teach our team to be 'on stage' while at work, we often don't know when someone is having a bad day. If I find out someone is going through a rough time, I try to do something special to show we care, such as sending flowers or a card, giving a service, or leaving a voice mail. By caring for the happiness of others, we cultivate a warm, friendly atmosphere that people are delighted to be part of. We really treat each other as family and do things to recognize each other's accomplishments. Our monthly team meetings often give us a chance to mention who inspires us. People often don't realize the impact they have on others. I am always flattered when people tell me I inspired them; when I ask how, it's usually because I suggested they try something or because I let them know I believed they could do it. Their response surprises me. I don't have unrealistic expectations of people; I sincerely believe they can do great things. I'm just getting them to believe it too."

## Creating Secret Service for your team

- Create definitive core values with which you measure potential employees.
- Work at creating a stronger corporate culture that dramatically reduces turnover.
- Define an Employee Experience Cycle, everything that does and can happen from the moment employees are interviewed until they retire. Add little Secret Service surprises to it that keeps up their morale and self-esteem.

- Create an orientation program that defines your story and legacy so that all new team members want to continue the heritage.
- Consider all the soft benefits that can be added, that don't necessarily cost a lot of money, but are thoughtful gestures to provide for your employees.

# CHAPTER 7

# An Opportunity to Be a Hero:

## Turning Customer Complaints into Positive Experiences

*Our strongest competition is our own reputation.*
*—Disney University*

A business theory states that if you please a customer, he will think well of you, but if you please a formerly disappointed customer, he will be your best source of advertising. A customer complaint is a chance for a company to be a hero. The best managers and well trained employees actively look for this kind of opportunity. They understand that customer challenges will arise. It's not that the best companies don't have crises; what sets them apart is that they have systems in place to rectify the problem immediately and make it appear never to have existed.

The best companies anticipate problems. Managers are like firefighters. Fires will happen every day; if there were no fires, we wouldn't need any managers. If your managers come to work without preparing for the eventuality of a fire, they should consider changing careers.

As both an employer and a customer, I have been involved in thousands of situations that didn't go as expected. This is the defining moment for a company. Nothing is a better indicator of how well a company trains its employees than how they respond to customer challenges.

One of my best examples of a company turning a negative experience into a positive one happened at Disney World. My son Johnni and I stood in line at Twilight Zone, a roller coaster at MGM Studios, for more than 50 minutes. When we finally got to the front of the line, the cast member stopped us and said Johnni was too small for the ride. He showed me the measuring stick and he was right. My son was almost 2 inches too short. The cast member apologized and said we must have missed the signs along the line. It was for my son's safety that he must be at least 40 inches in height. Who can argue with that? But after waiting in line for almost an hour for a ride he really wanted to go on, Johnni was about to cry.

Here was Disney at its finest. Disney employees did nothing wrong. It wasn't their fault we didn't pay attention to the signs explaining the size requirements, and they were only looking out for my son's safety. But the employee bent down to my teary-eyed son, asked his name, and said, "Johnni, I am going to give you a certificate with your name on it. This certificate says the next time you come to Disney, you will be tall enough to get on Twilight Zone and you won't have to wait in line. All you have to do is walk right up to the front of the line, show this certificate, and you'll go on the ride without waiting."

My son's expression turned into a smile. He felt like a Disney VIP. For the next 2 years that certificate hung on our refrigerator door, and every day Johnni said, "Can we go back to Disney World today?" I would measure him and say, "Not yet."

This is an example of a simple yet brilliant Secret Service system at work. That 19-year-old cast member became a hero, not only to my son but also to me, who faced having a very disappointed 6-year-old on my hands. Disney anticipated this because it had happened before, so they created a Secret Service system to rectify a potentially disappointing experience immediately, even when it's not Disney's fault.

## Anticipating Problems

It takes months to find a customer, and seconds to lose one.

—Eileen Brownell

Train your team to anticipate problems, both the ones that could be your fault and the ones that are not.

While closing a sale or at check-out, ask the client how everything was. If he or she says, "Fine," dig deeper because "fine" is like saying, "Let me pay and get out of here. It definitely was not what I was hoping for." It is critical that customers find it easy to express any dissatisfaction before they leave, because if they don't they will express it to everyone they can after they leave.

In the salon business we know that no matter how well we do, there will be times when an operator calls in sick and it's impossible to contact some of her clients. We also can expect there will be times when clients arrive and find their appointments are scheduled on another day or aren't on the book at all. No matter how well we train our team, we make thousands of appointments each year, and can make a human error.

John Robert's serves an average of 250 clients a day and 1,750 clients a week. If we make mistakes 1 percent of the time, this means at least 17 clients a week will be dissatisfied. So we train all our employees to fill out a guest challenge sheet any time they come across a client who is not completely satisfied. This way we can be proactive and follow up with the client to make sure the situation was resolved to her satisfaction. We put ourselves in a position to be a hero instead of leaving the client with a disappointment to share with friends and family.

John Robert's also trains its managers to scan faces in the salon during the day. Many situations can be avoided if we can catch them early enough. If we look for it, we can see the first traces of disappointment on a client's face. It may be someone in the experience room is getting frustrated because the hairdresser is running behind, or someone in a stylist's chair is beginning to feel her expectations are not being met. Perhaps the most challenging day is a homecoming or prom, when we are visited by more than 100 young teenage girls, who seem especially reluctant to tell the stylists what they really think. A good manager recognizes the signs of disappointment and maneuvers the situation to get the client's experience back on track.

The real key to success is empowering the team so that all employees at all levels can handle a situation as they think best. Many employers may fear that a lower level employee may be taken advantage of or will use poor judgment. I always tell my staff to err on the side of naïveté rather than paranoia. I would much rather be taken advantage of by a tiny minority of clients than insult and alienate the majority.

Many companies have policies in place that apply to about 2 percent of their clients and that insult the 98 percent who are good clients. An example is a sign saying, "A $20 fee will be charged to all clients whose checks are returned." The policy itself isn't wrong, but does it need to be advertised? We have found that any client who has bounced a check in our salon is typically a good client who made an honest mistake and has no problem paying any bank fees we incur.

## Empower the Team to Take Care of the Client

The best way to regain a lost client is not to lose that client in the first place.

We encourage our entire team to take care of any guest challenges as they see fit, without any fear of getting in trouble with management. We have created protocols to help guide our team in making a decision, but ultimately we believe that our staff can rely on their own instincts in rectifying the situation. We want every team member to look for opportunities to be a hero.

For example, if a client walks into our salon, says she is here for her 4:00 manicure with Denise, and we can't find any record of her appointment, then our protocol is put in place instantly. We don't make it the customer's problem by saying, "Sorry, we don't have you scheduled today." We become proactive and improvise quickly. First of all, we do not tell the client we don't have the appointment listed. In almost every instance we can still accommodate her, so she never needs to know that we made a mistake. Furthermore, if we were to tell her we didn't have her in the book and then are still able to accommodate her, she would still think we were incompetent.

If it's impossible for Denise to accommodate her, the person at the front desk explains to the client that there seems to be a mix-up, apologizes, and gives her choices, such as, "Lisa, who is an excellent manicurist, is available. If that doesn't work, Denise is available at 4:30

today." If the problem is rectified that easily, the employee at the front desk may thank the client sincerely for being so understanding and flexible, and nothing more may be needed.

If the client does not want Lisa to do her nails and cannot wait until 4:30, we offer her any other day and time with Denise at no charge. If we have absolutely no openings and the client needs the service that day, we call another salon, book an appointment, and pay for it ourselves.

## Speed Up the Process of Remedying Customer Dissatisfaction

Complaining clients are giving us the opportunity to make it right. It's the silent ones who worry me. They stay silent only until they get outside our door. Although no one enjoys addressing customers who are unhappy with our products or services, at least they are giving us the opportunity to fix the problem and reduce the damage. The ones who don't feel that it is worth discussing with us are the ones who never return and spread negative publicity.

Team members at any level must be empowered to handle the problem on the spot. If the problem gets past them, whether they handle it improperly or they lack the confidence and get a manager, it's too late. You have lost the client.

Every time that client tells the story of how you inconvenienced her, two things happen: She gets angrier, and the story becomes exaggerated. By the time a manager is called in and asks the client what happened, it may be the fourth or fifth time the client has told her story. Now she is really angry, and to justify it, she may embellish the story. Other clients may even overhear her.

It all could have been avoided if someone had handled it immediately. When you fix the situation right away, the client's opinion of your company rises, and she will be likely to tell everyone how professional you are. Clients understand that sometimes things go wrong. What really amazes clients is when you understand their plight and actually do something about it. You then have their loyalty for life, because they know that no matter what happens, you will make it right.

One of John Robert's hairdressers, Megan Godish, came to me one day to say that one of her good clients was really upset because we had gotten hair color on her blouse. Megan was very concerned about her client and wanted to be sure we made things right. I told Megan to tell the client we would pay for the cleaning, but Megan wanted me to call the client personally. I called the client, apologized, and said we would pay for any cleaning that the blouse needed. She said it could not be cleaned; the stain was permanent. I again apologized and said we would replace the blouse, but she said it was part of an outfit no longer available, and the outfit was worthless now that the blouse was ruined. I said we would send her a check that day for the cost of the outfit. She asked if I wanted to see the blouse, and I said it wasn't necessary. Then she asked if I wanted to see the receipt for the outfit, and I said that wasn't necessary either. Along with the check, we sent her a John Robert's gift certificate for the troubles and inconvenience that we had caused. This client continues to come to John Robert's and refers many people to us. She may be one of our best sources of advertising. Think of it this way: We could have run one newspaper ad that produced no clients whatsoever; we replaced one blouse and secured a customer for life.

## Be Sensitive to Client Expectations

When advertising hype sets the bar too high, you can only disappoint.

Training people to be proactive and sympathetic takes a lot of work and constant review. Your team members may see so many clients that it can become numbing. To prevent this, we train our team on clients' typical expectations. All clients come in with an idea of how they should be treated. The client who comes in with low expectations is typically the easiest to please. Usually this is a new client who had poor experiences at other establishments, so she views her visit not as an experience but more like a trip to the dentist's office. She expects a root canal and is pleasantly surprised. Because we have exceeded her expectations, we now have an enthusiastic fan. When a client comes in with very high expectations, the situation is very different. Usually this client has been referred to a company, has heard about the extras, and expects a perfect experience. If one thing goes wrong for just one moment, this client may be totally disappointed.

Remember: Although you may feel that your client is demanding, your competition won't.

## Practice Using Role Playing

Role playing is the best training to prepare for worst case scenarios. It also corrects the impression of most people that they have great customer service skills and are able to handle almost any situation. Put new employees in the role of dealing with a difficult situation. An excellent role playing exercise is "The Irrational Client." Here's how we do it at John Robert's: One employee plays the part of the employee and stands in front of the room. Everyone else is given a card describing the irrational client. Half of the cards describe the client as a man whose 4-year-old daughter was hit 3 days ago by an automobile and is still hospitalized in critical condition. The client hasn't left his child's side since the accident, and the doctor is scheduled to meet with the family at 1:00 P.M. Two weeks ago the client had made a 12:00 appointment with Patti, and he desperately needs a haircut. He figures that in 30 minutes he can run over to John Robert's, get a quick haircut and some much needed stress relief, and return to the hospital to meet with the doctor and be with his daughter.

The other half of the group receives cards describing the client as an arrogant attorney who called earlier the same day and demanded to be squeezed in at 12:00 for a haircut with Patti. He is usually late for his appointments and sometimes fails to show up.

As the role playing starts, the client walks up to the hostess and says, "I had a 12:00 with Patti. I checked in at noon, and it's now 12:15. Was someone going to inform me of this delay?"

The hostess responds, "I am so sorry, let me—"

"I am so tired of this place," the client says, interrupting her. "This is the third time in a row that I have waited at least 15 minutes."

"I apologize. I can see if Patti is ready for you."

Angry, the client says, "Ever since you guys were in that magazine and named the Best of Cleveland, it has gone to your heads."

The hostess is a little flustered. "Would it help if we reschedule your appointment with Patti for another time?"

Angrier now, the client says, "I called to see if Patti was running on time, and the person on the phone said she was. Now I have to wait. You have absolutely no respect for my time. You will never get a chance to treat me like this again." He storms out of the salon.

The role playing is over. We commend the new employee for her valiant effort, and we ask if anyone would have handled it differently.

The half whose cards describe an arrogant attorney feel the client was a bit unreasonable over the 15 minutes, possibly taking himself too seriously. The other half strongly disagree. They feel sympathy and compassion for the father of the critically injured child, and they want to do everything within their power to help him out. After some discussion between the two sides, we reveal what's written on the cards. The participants now understand the other side and realize how personal issues can impact a situation.

This scenario is not unrealistic. Considering how many clients we see in a day, a number of them have serious personal issues, even if we are unaware of it, and many people come to us for a brief escape. How much better our customer service would be if we handled every situation from that perspective. We would be more patient and understanding, and we would have many more satisfied clients.

From the standpoint of customer service, every company is only as strong as its weakest employee. Imagine going to a five-star restaurant and having a waiter who seems purposely to forget everything you ask for, and isn't there when you need him. Will you tell everyone how bad your waiter was? No, you'll probably tell people how terrible the restaurant was and suggest they avoid it.

A key factor that determines the quality of a company is that its employees make things right when given the chance to do so. As humans we are all bound to disappoint customers occasionally; what matters is how we respond.

## Turn Crises into Positive Experiences

Nearly every crisis ends up being helpful because it makes you refocus on something you had been neglecting.

I love the philosophy of Patrick Lally, owner of Tim Lally Chevrolet, of Bedford, Ohio. He says, "If a problem with a customer gets to me, it's free." This philosophy forces his managers to handle the situation because, as Patrick puts it, 'If I end up eating $2,000 or $3,000, it directly lowers that department's profit, which ultimately reduces the manager's bonus." It is no wonder why Tim Lally Chevrolet has been the #1 ranked Chevy dealership in customer service since 1997.

Cooker Bar and Grille Restaurants, with locations throughout the Midwest, aggressively seeks out dissatisfied customers. In an era when many organizations prefer to run and hide when they hear a customer isn't happy, Cooker does the opposite. They seek out their customers and make sure they are happy. If a customer is unhappy, Cooker rectifies the situation immediately. For example, if a customer has what Cooker's calls a "long greet," meaning the server took longer than expected to greet the party after they were seated, Cooker offers a complimentary dessert or even an entire meal. Cooker has a 100 percent satisfaction policy, printed right on the menu, stating that a customer who is unhappy with his meal doesn't have to pay for it. If Cooker finds out about a problem after a customer has paid, Cooker will give that customer a gift certificate good for the next visit. Molly Moody, a general manager in Ohio, explains Cooker's management philosophy: "If you make a table of five happy, they may tell 50 people; if you make one person unhappy, he may tell 500. We will overcompensate to rectify a situation." That kind of philosophy, followed up by systems that ensure the employees walk the talk, is refreshing in today's era of low customer service expectations.

## Enterprise Rent-A-Car

An excellent example of how to be proactive when you drop the ball is an incident in which an Enterprise Rent-A-Car, located in Massachusetts, didn't have a customer's reservation or vehicle available. Their customer service representative could have been skeptical that the reservation was never made by the customer; but instead apologized profusely and called nearby branches until they found the vehicle this customer needed. The service recovery mission didn't stop there. This Enterprise Rent-A-Car employee then drove the customer to the other branch to retrieve the vehicle, took 20% off the rental price, gave the customer $2 for a toll that he would not have had to pay had he left from the original branch, and gave him a half-tank of gas. Within a month, the customer had rented twice more from Enterprise.

An Enterprise Rent-A-Car based in St. Louis spends a significant amount of time tracking customer satisfaction and tying it to employee success. Only the "completely satisfied" customers count toward a particular branch's score. This ranking is a major factor in measuring potential for promotion. Like other great customer service companies, Enterprise employees are free to take steps that will make a customer happy, without having to go through bureaucratic approval and red tape. Because of that, Enterprise looks for and hires people who want to run their own business someday, and builds on that sense of initiative with an extensive employee training program.

## GOING ABOVE AND BEYOND

A salon's worst nightmare once happened to us. One of our designers inadvertently overprocessed a client's hair relaxer, damaging her hair so that it began to fall out. Our client was understandably distraught. We had to be honest and explain what we had done.

Our immediate concern was to try to make her feel comfortable about herself. She couldn't stand her hair: It was thinning, and what was left was damaged. Even though she was extremely unhappy with us, we convinced her to let us give her some treatments at no charge to try to strengthen her hair and reduce the breakage. After we styled her hair, she didn't hate it as much, and less hair seemed to fall out. We also gave her plenty of conditioning products to use at home, again at no charge. But nothing seemed to work. Despite all the treatments, products, and styling, her hair continued to break.

She said that all she wanted was her hair healthy. She didn't want money or services; she just wanted to feel good about herself again. I can't tell you how bad we felt for her. Initially, Stacy and I called her almost every night.

Besides giving her all these hair services and products for free, we gave her massages, facials, and pedicures. We sent her flowers, cards, and gift certificates to a restaurant. Before she went on vacation to Florida, she said she didn't know what she was going to do because she hated how her hair looked when she had to style it herself. So we offered to have a salon there style her hair, on us, of course. This continued for nearly a year. Over time she accepted the situation, and occasionally even laughed about it. Her hair got worse before it got better. Eventually, but not soon enough, it improved and returned to its original health.

This horrible event had a happy ending, not because of all the services and products we gave her, but because of the genuine concern we showed. In the beginning, I told her that I didn't care if she sued us; but I did want her to give us the chance to rectify it. Once it was rectified, I would understand if she never wanted to set foot in John Robert's again. I was willing to do anything we could to reduce her discomfort. We admitted our mistake immediately, were totally honest with her, and were willing to do anything we could to help her through this difficult time. We never made her feel she was inconveniencing us or overreacting, no matter how upset she was.

The client's hair improved, and she returned to John Robert's after the incident was resolved. She even referred people to us. We took a very unpleasant situation and turned it into an opportunity to shine. We obviously trained the designer to make sure she never made the mistake again.

## Creating Secret Service protocols for customer challenges

- Accept that you will have daily and recurring customer challenges and create a protocol that addresses them the moment they happen.
- Empower, train, and create a system for your employees so your team at every level is capable of addressing and resolving a customer complaint.

- Role play guest challenges and stereotypes your customers may have about doing business with you.
- Err on the side of being too aggressive handling customer challenges by taking the side of the customer. Show that you recognize their inconvenience and what you will do to make it right.

# CHAPTER 8

# Enhancing the Quality of Lives Around Us:

## Giving Back

The most selfless acts are the most rewarding.

Secret Service should extend to your customers, team, and also the community in which you do business. I have always marveled at the companies who shared their success with their communities and the pride it inspired in the people who worked there as well as the customers who chose to do business with them.

Since we opened, I knew that being involved in the community and giving back was going to be a critical part of the way we do business. I believe that giving back to the community also attracts employees who share these values. It surprises me that more businesses do not operate with similar philosophies. Although a certain amount of time and money is needed, the benefits far outweigh everything else.

First of all, you and your employees gain the sense of being an integral part of the community. Your staff and the entire organization are truly providing something of significant importance. Second, you cannot duplicate or quantify the amount of exposure this gives your organization and the light in which it is seen by the public and many potential customers. Such service will also increase the number of employee candidates who want to be part of such a company. Obviously many community involvement events also present good media opportunities.

When it's all said and done, building a strong community involvement presence generates trust, credibility, good will, name recognition, and employee and customer loyalty. Consider the following examples of corporate philanthropy.

## Blue Cross/Blue Shield

Blue Cross/Blue Shield of Minnesota has always been a major supporter of the American Red Cross, even before 9-11. Blue Cross employees have a 20-year tradition of donating blood to the Red Cross. Blue Cross also matches employee pledges to the United Way. In early 2001, they made a $100,000 grant to the American Red Cross stress team in Minnesota to provide counseling and professional help to victims of spring flooding and other natural disasters. Shortly after September 11, they committed $30,000 to support the American Red Cross in providing disaster relief in the wake of the terrorist attacks. The donation is part of a nationwide Blue Cross/Blue Shield effort to contribute $1 million to this cause.

## American Express

American Express is another leader in philanthropy. They have continuously had disaster relief programs, providing grants to the American Red Cross and other relief agencies. In addition they have sponsored AIDS Walks, raising funds for HIV education and prevention programs. American Express offers transitional housing, counseling, and outreach services to women and children who are victims of domestic violence. They also have a 3-year urban redevelopment project to revitalize East Lake in Atlanta, through the redevelopment of a troubled public housing project and creation of long-term educational, recreational, and social programs for residents.

In addition, they provide a program that improves reading skills by pairing corporate volunteers and New York elementary children. Their employees participate in building new homes to benefit low-income families in Dallas, Minneapolis, Phoenix, and other communities. American Express has aided expansion projects to improve operational efficiency of Houston Institute, which distributes food to more than 500 member agencies.

## Sprint

Sprint has established a reputation for active corporate citizenship and community leadership with commitments to programs such as donating a multi-million-dollar Asynchronous Transfer Mode network to link pediatric hospitals across the nation to a private computer network for hospitalized children. This interactive on-line community allows children to engage in entertaining and stimulating activities. They also can interact with peers facing similar challenges, share their own experiences, and help each other cope with the day-to-day realities of living with illness.

Sprint's Community Relations Teams have completed more than 4,000 community projects and logged more than 100,000 community service hours annually since 1997. Employee projects include refurbishing homes for elderly and disadvantaged people; collecting tons of food and thousands of gifts for people in need during the holiday season; participation in walks, runs, and bike rides; and working with schools to build playgrounds and provide expertise in classrooms.

## Ben & Jerry's

Ben & Jerry's is well known for their ice cream and frozen yogurt, but what they may be equally known for is their Ben & Jerry's Foundation, which is a corporate role model for community involvement. The mission of the Ben & Jerry's Foundation is to make the world a better place by empowering Ben & Jerry's employees to use available resources to support and encourage organizations that are working toward eliminating the underlying causes of environmental and social problems.

The Ben & Jerry's Foundation was established in 1985 and makes yearly donations of more than $1.1 million dollars. An employee-led Community Action Team runs this foundation. The Ben & Jerry's Foundation offers competitive grants to not-for-profit, grassroots organizations throughout the United States that facilitate progressive social change by addressing the underlying conditions of societal and environmental problems. All of the Foundation's funding decisions are made by a team of Ben & Jerry's employees that meets three times a year to review proposals.

## Adobe

The Adobe Software company donates software to nonprofit organizations and K–12 schools as free software training courses focus on teaching educators how to use Adobe products to bring technology into the classroom.

## Microsoft

Bill Gates and Microsoft have taken some huge hits as a corporate bully, but the Seattle-based software company foundation has endowed more than $24 billion in grants that focus on expanding access to technology through public libraries and improving global health.

## John Robert's

Being an integral part of the community is a huge part of John Robert's philosophy. From the beginning, our mission has been to "enhance the quality of lives around us." We feel that it is critical to give back to our community. We emphasize, even to potential team members during their first interview, how much we do and how much it's part of our culture.

You cannot be all things to all people. If you are a small company, you will have to focus on one specific group to make any real impact. Our team at John Robert's chose children in need as our sole focus. We feel that children need to have their lives touched in a positive way, especially those who are hospitalized with a serious illness and children who are disadvantaged or abused.

As part of giving back, in November and December we display a sharing wreath in our salons for all the children who will spend the holidays at Rainbow Babies & Children's Hospital in Cleveland. The wreath displays each child's name and age and what gift he or she would like for the holidays. Clients choose a name, purchase the gift, and bring it in to us. The first Christmas Eve, we took a trunk full of gifts to Rainbow. The second year we needed a mini-van. Now we need a full-size van, and we hope to need a truck eventually. It's wonderful to see these children's faces light up when they see so many presents. We received this letter in 1995 after a station televised our staff dropping off the presents given by our clients:

*Dear Mr. & Mrs. DiJulius:*

*My husband and I saw the news feature last night about the donations of toys to Rainbow Babies & Children's Hospital. Last Christmas, our 11-year-old son Ezrah was a patient there. He received some very nice gifts and we believe some of them came from your efforts. Unfortunately, our son passed away on January 15 after being diagnosed with leukemia on December 23. It is very difficult to face this Christmas without him. However, we decided it would be nice to give a donation to help some other child have a nice Christmas. The toys and games he received really boosted his spirits, and we'd like to be part of helping some other child have a more enjoyable Christmas. We don't have much to give, but we know this donation [$10] will be put to good use. May God bless you both for the love you're showing.*

> *Sincerely,*
> *Mr. & Mrs. Robert L. Johnson*

We're not here to just take money out of the community; we are here to enhance it.

At noon on every New Year's Eve, we sponsor a holiday party at Rainbow Babies & Children's Hospital. On one of these occasions, a nurse remarked, "This is very nice. It's unfortunate that during the other 11 months of the year these kids are forgotten."

That prompted our team to decide to visit the children at Rainbow once a month. In 1995, on the second Monday of every month, we began sending two or three of our team members to Rainbow to provide services for patients. Our team members paint nails and provide hand-and-arm massages. For children who still have hair, we cut, style, and braid it. If a teenage girl is losing or has lost her hair, we help her self-esteem by giving her a John Robert's beret and teaching her how to wear makeup. Most of us cannot imagine what it's like to be a 15-year-old girl with absolutely no hair. The nurses tell us that many of these kids don't even get out of bed until they have to, but on the days they know we are coming, they get so excited that they're up and ready, bright and early.

We came to realize that these children are constantly getting shots and being tested and prodded. It is rare and so nice to have someone come and touch them in a positive way by pampering them. We instantly saw their morale improve. Our staff gets so much out of this, because not only do we feel we are enhancing the quality of these children's lives, but we also realize how fortunate we and our families are.

One thing overwhelmed me the first time I went to Rainbow. I couldn't begin to imagine what it must be like to be a parent of one these children. I saw all these parents staying at the hospital night after night, putting the rest of their lives on hold, trying to be a source of strength for their child, hoping and praying for a miracle. I wanted to be able to do something for these parents. At that point we decided to give the mothers of terminally ill children a Mother's Day gift of a day of pampering at John Robert's. These moms sleep countless nights at the hospital, for months at a time. We wanted to give them a rare but well-deserved opportunity for a few hours of pampering and nurturing. We let the nurses select the moms, and the week before Mother's Day we have a limousine bring them to John Robert's for a few hours of respite.

We are proud of our Prom Promise Haircuts, which we have provided at local high schools every spring since 1994, after some tragic accidents that resulted from teenagers drinking and driving on prom night. We visit each high school and give a complimentary haircut to every senior who signs the John Robert's Prom Promise Contract: "I will not drink or drive, or participate with anyone who does." A parent and the principal must also sign it. We know a few students may do this for a free haircut, but we feel that the importance of the contract is reinforced by having the student, principal, and parent all sign it. We also hand out pins saying, "I signed the John Robert's Prom Promise Contract," and information from insurance companies on the staggering fatal statistics that result from drinking and driving.

Many businesses relax their dress code on Fridays. When John Robert's does this, it's with the stipulation that employees donate a minimum of $5 to a specified charity or cause. In these and many other individual instances, our team gives back to the community. The real score card for success records the number of people's lives you have improved.

I was never so proud to have a credit card from any company as I was a few days after September 11. When I called Chase Credit Card, I heard this announcement: "We are concerned about our customers during this national crisis and have flexible policies to address any resulting hardships you may have." Many businesses would never have thought to be so proactive, for fear that people might take advantage of them.

We participate in Project Day-Maker, a nonprofit organization founded in 1995 by Frederic Holzberger, President and CEO of Fredric's Corporation. Project Day-Maker is a 34-foot Winnebago "Salon on Wheels" that goes to homeless shelters and treatment centers across the United States, providing haircuts and beauty care, literally touching the lives of abused children, battered women, and the homeless. Salon owners and stylists volunteer their time and services to help rebuild clients' self-esteem, ultimately assisting them back into the workforce. Project Day-Maker has contributed 5,000-plus haircuts.

John Beltzer, a professional recording artist, began Songs of Love Foundation with the mission to write, sing, and produce personalized songs for terminally and chronically ill children. This amazing concept has caught on, and outside funding has enabled Songs of Love to produce thousands of songs, each written for a specific child. These songs inspire these children and help get them and their families through difficult times. Best of all, there is no charge to a family for their child's personalized song. I can't think of a better example of enhancing the quality of life.

### Creating Secret Service for your community

- Determine the area where you can make the biggest impact. Obviously you cannot be all things to all people; it's better to have a a bigger impact on a few instead of a smaller impact on many. Let it be your staff's decision.
- Make giving back a core value that every potential team member possesses.
- Train and educate your staff on the benefits of giving back.

- Consider whether there are any areas that your services, products, and expertise can affect and benefit your community.
- Create a community event schedule in which you are repeatedly involved at certain times of the year, rotating staff involvement.
- Get the media involved.
- Network to get other business leaders and their companies involved.
- Get the word out what your company does to the customer base, suppliers, employees, and others.

# CHAPTER 9

# E-nough:
## Getting Back to Face-to-Face Relationships

Even though technology can simplify things, deliver products and services more quickly, and make us more productive, it will never give us the warm and fuzzy feeling that comes from sincerity, trust, and courtesy.

While buying books on Amazon.com one night, I came across titles such as e-conomy, e-college, e-business, e-conomics, and e-volve, to name just a few books on the crest of the Internet wave. Now, you won't find a person who loves technology more than I do, but I fear that our hi-tech society—especially our younger generation—is becoming less exposed to face-to-face interaction, and our people skills are slowly eroding.For example, houses built 50 to 60 years ago had beautiful front porches. People enjoyed hanging out at night on their front porches and socializing with dozens of neighbors. Today our society has moved in the totally opposite direction. People began building their porches and decks at the back of the house, and moving out to more rural areas for more land and privacy. Besides the computer gaining so much popularity with the younger generations, so many more games are available today, such as Playstation, Nintendo, CD ROMs, DVDs, and so on. Children aren't outside playing and interacting with each other as in previous generations. Many communities have seen a large decline in the number of children signing up for

155

recreational sports. Using technology to improve efficiencies and productivity is walking a gray line. Although these advances ultimately
should benefit the consumer, in some cases we need to examine impersonal aspects that the customer may feel and react to negatively. Today
companies are even advertising the fact that if you call them a live person will answer the phone.

Sometimes it's just evolutional change that the consumer is having trouble dealing with and will eventually adapt to, but in these
cases, it's not always beneficial to be a pioneer. Those who test and introduce the new technology first will take the most criticism for getting away from the personal touch. Like many people, I have seen a
big decline in customer service over the past 5 years. A strong economy allowed people and companies to be less responsive to customers'
needs because the demand exceeded the capacity to handle it. I don't
blame the decline in customer service on technology or on the Internet, but they aren't helping the situation. For example, if I can buy
something online, I do. I no longer go to bookstores; I order online at
11:30 P.M. The Internet is very convenient and offers many advantages, but it also reduces the amount of face-to-face interaction that
I had in the past. I haven't set foot in a bank for more than 3 years; I
have direct deposit, and I can go online to view my accounts, transfer
funds, and pay bills. All these great conveniences have eliminated the
need to talk to people.

Companies are always struggling with the dilemma of implementing cost savings with technological advances. An excellent example of this is self-checkout scanners that many retailers are using more
and more. Many pros and cons obviously need to be weighed: saving
money versus giving up customer service, reducing payroll versus up-
setting your corporate culture and compromising employee loyalty,
and reducing long check-out lines versus an impersonal systematic
customer relationship.

Target, a national retailer based in Minneapolis, which operates
990 stores, decided against investing in self-checkout scanners after
surveying its customers. Their guests strongly preferred to have human
interaction. For the most part, Target found out that their customers
appreciate the service they get from cashiers. Many companies that put

these self-scanners in, in hopes of reducing payroll, find that they are giving up more service than their customers appreciate.

Wal-Mart is testing self-checkout scanners in a few of its 2,600 stores. Some say the rush to embrace self-checkout is premature. The premise is that your customers will benefit because they won't have to wait in line anymore. Although there are many reasons why self-checkout scanners would be great, many like Wal-Mart are taking a crawl–walk–run approach. The problems have more to do with human psychology than technology. The grocery industry drastically reduced payroll when they cut back on bag boys and turned that responsibility over to their customers, who bag their own groceries. Many people have trouble bagging groceries or don't want to. One other major obstacle, retailers are finding out, is that many customers are extremely intimidated not only by new technology, but also by technology of any type.

Obvious benefits are that such a process can cut down on the hiring of cashiers and baggers, salaries, and employee benefits. Kroger, a national grocerer, is cautious when it comes to labor costs. Unlike Houston-based Randalls Food Markets, Inc., Kroger does not guarantee that all registers will be manned during peak hours. Randall officials say they are eyeing the technology, but will wait and see how competitors fare. Randall feels that their business is still too dependent on the human touch, realizing that many still like shopping the old-fashioned way.

Although technology makes it much easier to obtain information, it frequently comes at the price of poorer people-skills and customer service. Technology can be very beneficial if used in a nonobtrusive way. Databases for keeping track of customer preferences, for example, can greatly improve your customer service.

## Swiss

Swiss, a new Swiss intercontinental airline, has launched a customer relationship management software to help improve its targeted marketing campaigns and raise customer satisfaction. The airline has put all its customer data, collected from travel agent systems, website interaction, and call centers, into one centralized database, which stores historical flight information, sales and marketing data, and customer preferences. This allows the airline to segment its customer and target marketing campaigns to each specific group.

This has improved the airline's customer loyalty and frequent flyer programs. By tracking customer segments to their individual interests, the airline can provide offers to their customers that match their interests. In addition they can be a value-added resource; for instance, if they know a customer enjoys golf, Swiss could send them an offer from a golf club partner. They can package flights with car rentals, hotel offers, and vacation packages, thus creating a larger pie for the entire travel industry.

## JCPenney

JCPenney Direct Marketing Services, which markets supplemental insurance products and membership clubs through telemarketing, has made its customer service call center more efficient by installing interactive voice response technology, which has freed up its agents to handle more complicated customer inquiries while preserving customers' satisfaction levels.

The system identifies customers by their home telephone number; the automatic number identification system recognizes the origin of the call and immediately pulls up the policy history of the person making the call. If the system does not recognize the number, the customer is then asked to key in his or her home phone number.

Based on information JCPenney has collected about the nature of its customers' calls at certain times in their life cycle as policyholders, the system can determine whether the person is likely to have a question that will require an agent. If it is determined that the caller's needs can be met by the handful of simple questions that can be answered using the telephone keypad, the call is routed into the interactive voice response system.

This technology has been implemented successfully without sacrificing the personal service associated with live agents. The company polled its customers and found their satisfaction levels were just as high as when they were going through a live agent. This system handles more than 30,000 calls a month. The technology is helping the company keep costs down as the service centers grow.

We have also seen banks and credit card companies implement a similar automated attendant, which has deferred as many as 50 to 70 percent of their calls because most are inquires, such as determining account balances that can be accomplished easily through the automated attendant.

These are examples of how technology can improve service, but make sure you don't make service sacrifices when implementing technology. When contemplating implementing technology advances ask yourself the following:

1. How important are one-on-one relationships to my customers and is the success of my business dependent on them?
2. What will the short term personal perception be to my customers?
3. While it may eliminate jobs, will it eliminate customers?
4. Has this worked successfully in other businesses?
5. Are we giving the perception to our customers and employees that we are too corporate and bureaucratic now than before?

If after answering these questions you find that using a new technology was a mistake, don't be afraid to retract it. First Union, the nation's sixth largest bank, realized the importance of customer intimacy and quickly corrected themselves. The bank recently annoyed some if its customers when it tried to get them to rely less on tellers and more on banking by computer and phone. When First Union realized that its "future bank" concept was a mistake, it quickly hired 2,000 more tellers.

## New Technology May Actually Hurt Sales

Many companies succumb to the technology boom and forget that automation doesn't always make life easier for customers or give them what they want. When we built a facility of 8,000 square feet, we purchased a $20,000 phone system that could do everything for us but make coffee. Of course I wanted to justify the expense, and one of the ways to do that was to have an automatic caller distribution system (ACD) answer and distribute all our incoming calls.

I estimated that at least 20 to 30 percent of our calls were for reasons other than scheduling an appointment. The personnel in our call center spent a great deal of their time answering questions about our hours, giving the phone number of our salon in Solon, or forwarding messages. So I liked the idea of having an ACD filter our incoming calls.

The caller got an automated attendant saying, "If you want to schedule an appointment, hit 1. If you know your party's extension, dial it now. If you would like to reach our corporate offices, hit 2. If you would like to reach our Solon salon, hit 3." It was a perfect system, and our company and clients would benefit. By reducing the call center's number of incoming calls that had nothing to do with appointments, our call center's staff could focus on people calling for appointments, thus giving better service and reducing hold times. Everyone would win. Right? Wrong.

It didn't work out that way at all.

Stacy disapproved of the idea from day one, and she told me our customers would also. After we rolled the system out, she kept telling me how many complaints we were getting, but I stubbornly stuck to my thinking. ACD was the right way for a company to operate. The customer must be flexible because this was the way things were done now. I was certain that we just needed time to perfect the system. We didn't have the call centers staffed correctly.

It never got any better; actually, it got worse. I know we lost more customers because of our phone system than for any other reason. Most people ignored all the prompts and hit 1, for an appointment, regardless of the reason for their call because they knew they would get a human. This didn't work, however, because everyone at the call center was already tied up with phone calls, and as a result the caller got another recording, "Due to the increase in call volume, you may be briefly placed on hold. Your call will be taken in the order in which it was received." Going from one message to another was like being trapped in a voice-mail maze, which upset our clients even more. Before ACD, people had not minded being put on hold, but the ACD sent them from an automated attendant to another message and left them on hold again.

I knew it was really bad when I wouldn't call my own salon because I didn't like how long I was kept on hold. Our phone system became our biggest and most common complaint. Our clients felt we were becoming too big. We no longer appeared to be the intimate salon and spa that had made us so successful.

We went back to answering the phones as soon as they rang and eliminated ACD completely. We also added more staff to our call center, which helped a great deal. When a human began answering the phones again, our complaints and hold times decreased almost immediately, and we were once again viewed as personal and intimate. We even announced the change in a newsletter, hoping that the clients we had put off would see it and give us another try.

## Don't Rely on Classes Alone

We believe that our team members are as important as our clients. Many businesses hold classes on customer service but neglect to relate it to the co-worker. Customer service is assumed to be a matter of common sense, but common sense, as mentioned in an earlier chapter, is uncommon. John Robert's has implemented the Wal-Mart principle that any time an employee is within 10 feet of a customer, he greets the customer. Equally important, we also do this with each other, our team members. After all, we may walk past one another half a dozen times each day. Why not say hi with a smile? Nothing is more deflating than to be in a good mood and to have a co-worker bring you down. When we make our team more aware of providing great customer service skills to each other, we don't have to worry about how our team takes care of the guests. It snowballs. Morale improves, customer service improves, and client retention improves. Hal Becker says it best in his book *Lip Service:* "Having customer service seminars only once a year for your people is like deodorant. It wears off after a while and the old smell comes back again. Customer service training has to be their focus every day."

## Be Aware of How Our Social Skills Have Declined

The next time you're out, stop and notice what people do and don't do. Start by letting another car go ahead of you in busy traffic, and see if you receive a wave as a gesture of thanks. Or stop at an intersection and pull up a bit so the car behind you can make a right turn. Does the driver wave a thank you? As you go through a doorway, hold the door for a stranger walking behind you, and see if he thanks you as he passes. The next time you are the one following a stranger through a door, maybe with your hands full, notice if he thinks to hold it open for you. Ask ten people today, "How are you doing?" and see how many just reply, "Fine," or "Good," without saying, "I'm doing well, thanks. How are you?" When you use the drive-through at a fast-food chain or exit a parking garage, see if you are thanked after you pay.

Now that you are more aware of these things, you may be shocked to learn how often you will be disappointed in the outcome of these experiments, that we no longer give and get what used to be common courtesy. Our expectations of customer service are very low today; we just hope that the day doesn't bring a horror story.

That's why I am so lucky to be in the salon-and-spa business. People need us more than ever, not because they need hair color or a massage to relieve the stress. They need us because we are a commodity that still makes them feel good and that they cannot get on the Internet.

To a certain degree, the salon industry is recession proof. When the economy slows, the big-ticket items suffer: new home purchases, additions to the house, new cars, and vacations. But people will continue to purchase the small amenities that provide immediate benefits, especially when excellent customer service is given. People get choosy about where they spend their money during slower times. In 2001 the U.S. economy had been experiencing a slowdown for more than a year, but John Robert's business was up almost 40 percent. So far my theory has been supported by our numbers.

## Being Successful in a Difficult Economy

Even a turkey can fly in a tornado.

—*Eugene Kleiner*

A sluggish economy is not the worst thing that can happen. Although it's unpleasant to see companies go out of business and people get laid off, a slower economy does weed out the poor businesses (turkeys) that were flying high in a great economy (tornado). When the economy slows, consumers give their business only to those companies that have earned it.

In the past, many companies benefited from a very strong economy regardless of whether or not they provided good customer service. If I complained to a restaurant manager about a problem, the response often was, "Buddy, look around. Do you see how busy we are?" The message was: Your complaint doesn't really matter.

The salon and spa industry is not the only industry that should be even more attractive to consumers today. In *Pour Your Heart into It*, Starbucks CEO Howard Schultz talks about how Starbucks has been so successful because cafes are a third place that our society desperately needs today. For most people past their 20s, life consists of work and home, but that isn't enough. We need to be able to go to places where we can interact with others. Once you're out of the dating scene and no longer see great value in nightlife in bars, your social interaction with others drastically diminishes. Offering a place for social contact explains the popularity of cafes in the United States in the past decade.

The same can also be said for health clubs, restaurants, retail stores, malls, vacation resorts, hotels, hardware stores, grocery stores, and dry cleaners. The businesses that understand this fact incorporate it into their branding and market it to their existing and potential clients, and will flourish.

Businesses not only have to look at barriers with their customers that reduce the personal touch, but also at barriers internal with their own employees. As corporations grow and add layers of departments, red tape and bureaucracy inevitably is created and many times employees start to feel like a number, or part of the herd instead. Jack Welch, one of the most admired CEOs of the twentieth century, fought a two-decade war against bureaucracy. He coined phrases such as boundaryless and workout as tools to address his intolerance of bureaucracy, and stressed the importance of building an organization of trust, excitement, and informality. The former GE leader recognized the adverse effects of bureaucracy and knew unless his company tackled it head on and greatly reduced it, GE would never become a worldwide leader in their markets.

Some initiatives Welch took were to make sure that those who did the work got a say in how the business could run better. He also got his leadership team to recognize all great ideas did not have to come from GE. GE would bring people of all ranks and functions—managers, secretaries, engineers, line workers, customers, and suppliers—into a room to focus on a problem. Then the company would act rapidly on the best ideas.

So e-nough. Reinstitute face-to-face interactions that help us create relationships and connect with people. And e-nough with tolerating marginal customer service or giving marginal customer service. And e-nough with not hearing, "Thank you," "May I help you," and, "It would be my pleasure." The businesses that provide face-to-face inter-actions with the public have an enormous edge over everyone else.

All this decline in creating a relationship with the consumer has created an opportunity for those companies that are prepared to make it their point of difference. The few that continue to seek out every opportunity to make their customers feel like Norm did when he walked into Cheers, recognize them by name, utilize their database to personalize the experience, provide value-added to exceed their ex-pectations, and ultimately deliver unforgettable customer service will capitalize greatly on what so many people are yearning for and gravi-tating back to.

While the 1990s were about who can provide service the fastest and most conveniently at any cost, I think the 2000s will be about cre-ating relationships again, as it was back in the days of the hardware store, the barber shop, and the butcher shop. We knew their owners and enjoyed how we felt when we did business with them. They knew us by name and seemed genuinely glad to see us. And the companies that create Secret Service systems to earn customer confidence and loy-alty will be the companies that experience the most growth and oppor-tunities in their marketplace.

**Creating Secret Service to enhance and create relationships again**

- Consider how you can make each customer interaction more per-sonal, whether you're relying on a database for customer prefer-ences, remembering significant things about them, and so on.

- Create strong training and systems that teach your staff to recall things and utilize this personal information to personalize your customer's experience.
- Make your staff aware of how our society has deteriorated in terms of building one to one relationships, how people are yearning for it again, and how there is a huge opportunity for those who do capitalize on it.
- Before implementing any technology advances, regardless of their efficiencies, consider the impact it will make with your consumer and staff as far as their perception of how personal you are as a company.

# Index

# About the Author

In just 10 years (1993–2003), John DiJulius has grown John Robert's Hair Studio & Spa from one employee and zero sales to 130 employees and more than $4 million in annual sales. John Robert's has 750 to 1,000 new clients per month and retains 70 percent of its new clients (the industry average is 35 percent).

These results have been achieved through the principles of Secret Service, which John adapted from the best practices in all industries. John and his wife, Stacy, have three salon and spa locations, in Mayfield, Solon, and Chagrin Falls, Ohio. In addition to John Robert's Hair Studio & Spa, John is also the president of Minding Your Business, a business consulting firm, that takes him across the United States as a speaker and consultant on customer service and marketing.

John has a B.B.A. (Bachelor of Business Administration) in Marketing from Cleveland State University.

## Honors and Awards

- One of the top 200 salons in the United States five years in a row (1997–2001) by *Salon Today Magazine.*
- Voted Best Salon of Cleveland by *Cleveland Magazine.*

- Ernst & Young Entrepreneur of the Year Award (1999).
- One of the 100 fastest growing companies in Cleveland, five years in a row (1998–2001), by Weatherhead School of Management, Case Western Reserve University.
- One of the top 99 companies to work for in Northeast Ohio (1999–2002), by Employers Resource Council & Enterprise Development, Inc.
- Pillar Award from *Small Business News* (1999) for community service in Northeast Ohio.
- Northeast Ohio Success Award from *Inside Business Magazine* for top performing companies in Northeast Ohio three years in a row (1999–2001).
- Leadership Excellence Award from the American Society for Training and Development.

## Secret Service II

Have your own Secret Service systems? Send them to us to be included in our future *Secret Service* books!

For more information, or to reach John DiJulius, see the author's website, www.secretservicesystems.com or visit him at www.john robertsspa.com or e-mail him at jdijulius@johnrobertsspa.com.